JAMES
JOYCE

COMPREHENSIVE RESEARCH
AND STUDY GUIDE

BLOOM'S
MAJOR
NOVELISTS

EDITED AND WITH AN
INTRODUCTION BY HAROLD BLOOM

JAMES
JOYCE

EDITED AND WITH AN INTRODUCTION
BY HAROLD BLOOM

© 2002 by Chelsea House Publishers, a subsidiary of
Haights Cross Communications.

Introduction © 2002 by Harold Bloom.

Printed and bound in the United States of America.

First Printing
1 3 5 7 9 8 6 4 2

Library of Congress Cataloging-in-Publication Data
James Joyce / edited and with an introduction by Harold Bloom.
        p. cm.—(Bloom's major novelists)
    Includes bibliographical references and index.
    ISBN 0-7910-6353-4 (alk. paper)
    1. Joyce, James, 1882–1941—Criticism and interpretation.
  2. Ireland—In literarture. I. Bloom, Harold. II. Series.
  PR6019.O9 Z6335 2001
  823'.912—dc21   2001047499

Chelsea House Publishers
1974 Sproul Road, Suite 400
Broomall, PA 19008-0914

The Chelsea House World Wide Web address is
http://www.chelseahouse.com

Series Editor: Matt Uhler

Contributing Editor: Portia Williams Weiskel

Produced by Publisher's Services, Santa Barbara, California

Contents

User's Guide

This volume is designed to present biographical, critical, and bibliographical information on the author's best-known or most important works. Following Harold Bloom's editor's note and introduction is a detailed biography of the author, discussing major life events and important literary accomplishments. A plot summary of each novel follows, tracing significant themes, patterns, and motifs in the work.

A selection of critical extracts, derived from previously published material from leading critics, analyzes aspects of each work. The extracts consist of statements from the author, if available, early reviews of the work, and later evaluations up to the present. A bibliography of the author's writings (including a complete list of all works written, cowritten, edited, and translated), a list of additional books and articles on the author and his or her work, and an index of themes and ideas in the author's writings conclude the volume.

~

Harold Bloom is Sterling Professor of the Humanities at Yale University and Henry W. and Albert A. Berg Professor of English at the New York University Graduate School. He is the author of over 20 books, including *Shelley's Mythmaking* (1959), *The Visionary Company* (1961), *Blake's Apocalypse* (1963), *Yeats* (1970), *A Map of Misreading* (1975), *Kabbalah and Criticism* (1975), *Agon: Toward a Theory of Revisionism* (1982), *The American Religion* (1992), *The Western Canon* (1994), and *Omens of Millennium: The Gnosis of Angels, Dreams, and Resurrection* (1996). *The Anxiety of Influence* (1973) sets forth Professor Bloom's provocative theory of the literary relationships between the great writers and their predecessors. His most recent books include *Shakespeare: The Invention of the Human,* a 1998 National Book Award finalist, and *How to Read and Why,* which was published in 2000.

Professor Bloom earned his Ph.D. from Yale University in 1955 and has served on the Yale faculty since then. He is a 1985 MacArthur Foundation Award recipient, served as the Charles Eliot Norton Professor of Poetry at Harvard University in 1987–88, and has received honorary degrees from the universities of Rome and Bologna. In 1999, Professor Bloom received the prestigious American Academy of Arts and Letters Gold Medal for Criticism.

Currently, Harold Bloom is the editor of numerous Chelsea House volumes of literary criticism, including the series BLOOM'S NOTES, BLOOM'S MAJOR DRAMATISTS, BLOOM'S MAJOR NOVELISTS, MAJOR LITERARY CHARACTERS, MODERN CRITICAL VIEWS, MODERN CRITICAL INTERPRETATIONS, and WOMEN WRITERS OF ENGLISH AND THEIR WORKS.

Editor's Note

My Introduction meditates upon what I consider to be Stephen's waning as a personality in *Ulysses*, compared to his vividness in *A Portrait of the Artist as a Young Man.*

As there are eighteen critical extracts on the *Portrait*, and nineteen in *Ulysses*, I will comment briefly only upon some I have found of particular interest.

Derek Attridge, one of the most comprehensive of Joyce's scholars, capably introduces the study of Joyce, after which aspects of the artist in Stephen are explored by Harry Levin and Richard Ellmann. Karen Lawrence usefully addresses herself to the Joycean view of women.

The dramatist Thornton Wilder introduces the universality of *Ulysses*. For wide-ranging insights into the novel, S. L. Goldberg, Robert Martin Adams, and Umberto Eco seem to me outstanding.

Introduction

HAROLD BLOOM

The fragmentary *Stephen Hero* can be judged to present a more sympathetic Stephen Daedalus (as it is spelled there) than the Stephen Dedalus of *A Portrait* and *Ulysses*. Young Daedalus has more of Joyce's own humor and more capacity for Paterian aesthetic ecstasy than Dedalus will manifest. And yet critics are accurate in seeing Stephen in *A Portrait* as a considerable advance in representation upon *Stephen Hero*. The protagonist of *A Portrait* is naturalistically persuasive, a considerable improvement upon David Copperfield, Dickens's mixed portrait of the novelist as a young man. When Stephen Dedalus appears again in *Ulysses*, he necessarily loses the naturalistic and symbolist center to Poldy. But then, Leopold Bloom is one of a double handful of novelistic personages who possess something like Shakespearean inwardness and complexity of spirit.

Joyce's scholars, with rare exceptions, undervalue Walter Pater, which seems to me foolish and misleading. Stephen in *A Portrait* is Paterian in the best sense: his epiphanies give evidence of the power of the artist over a universe of death. Harry Levin finds Stephen's gift to be the attachment of "literary associations with sense impressions of the moment," which is to follow Pater's project. Hugh Kenner, the High Modernist critic, savaged Stephen as "indigestably Byronic." I don't wish to argue digestions, but Shelley and Pater are far closer to Stephen than was George Gordon, Lord Byron. An ironic reading of *A Portrait* leaves one in the position of Wallace Stevens's Mrs. Alfred Uruguay, who has wiped away moonlight like mud. Stephen is the positive culmination of Pater's vision of the aesthetic consciousness heroically sustaining itself against the flux of sensations. T. S. Eliot (who disliked Pater) is not the author of *A Portrait of the Artist as a Young Man*, though you could not know this by reading some of Joyce's critics. Derek Attridge, in my view, gets Joyce right when he sees him fundamentally as a great naturalistic writer, with realism outweighing the symbolist component. Yet that is precisely the importance of Walter Pater, as much a master of reality-testing as was Sigmund Freud (who admired Pater). Stephen's epiphanies are borrowed from Pater's privileged moments, which are Hamletian bursts of radiance against the darkening background of entropic death-drive. Stephen's heroism in *A Portrait* is precisely Paterian: we have a moment, and then our place knows us no more. The Gospel of Pater teaches perception and sensation, in the predicate that there is nothing more. What is there, in *Ulysses* and *Finnegans Wake,* that transcends perception and sensation? Eliot and Kenner tried to baptize Joyce's imagination, but that, as William Empson emphasized, is to create a mockery of Joyce's lifelong rejection of Roman Catholicism and its "hangman God."

To read *A Portrait* accurately, you need to accept Stephen as a Paterian hero of consciousness, akin to Oscar Wilde or to Pater's own Sebastian Van Storck in his *Imaginary Portraits.* The artist perceives for us, and expands our sensations because, as Nietzsche observed of Hamlet, he thinks not too much but too well. We possess art, according to Pater as to Nietzsche, lest we perish of the truth. Stephen is heroic in *A Portrait* because he intends to go into exile, lest he die of Irish truth. If, in *Ulysses,* Stephen is less persuasive, it is because he has not yet departed into Joyce's permanent exile.

The advent of the twenty-first century clarifies even more precisely that Proust and Joyce, Kafka and Beckett, were the inescapably narrative writers of the twentieth century, compared to whom even such figures as Mann, Lawrence, and Faulkner are secondary. If you regard Freud as a narrative master, he might rival Joyce and Proust, but he was most himself as a moral essayist, more akin to Montaigne and Emerson. Stephen matters in the way the unnamed "Marcel" matters in Proust's vast saga: these are heroes in search of lost time. Pater was an authority on lost time, as was Freud.

When we encounter Stephen again in *Ulysses,* we are saddened because of the waning of his energy. Joyce seems almost content to lose his earlier self to time, while finding himself again in Poldy's curiosity and humane universalism. *Ulysses* might indeed be called *A Portrait of the Artist as a Middle-aged Man.* Poldy seems to me even more of a triumph of representation than much of our criticism acknowledges. Is there a literary character in his century who is his equal? Proust's consciousness is so vast that his narrator cannot grow into it until the closing pages, but Poldy is altogether there from the start. It is too late to quarrel with Joyce's paradigm of *Ulysses,* but Poldy, though an exile and endlessly shrewd, is never cunning or sly. As Joyce was an admirable personage, so indeed is his

Poldy: he is morally and imaginatively superior to everyone else in the book. There is more than a bit of the artist in him: he incarnates not only kindness and goodness, but high art's vision of reality.

So strong and complex is Poldy's personality that Stephen's fades in contrast. Anthony Burgess based his portrait of Shakespeare, in *Nothing Like the Sun,* on both Stephen Dedalus and Leopold Bloom, but more on Bloom, though Burgess's Shakespeare, another lover of peace and abhorrer of violence, exists in a time and place that Poldy could not have sustained.

The largest mistake one could make about Poldy is to consider him ordinary. My experience of "ordinary" men and women is that they are likely to be quite ruthless. Poldy is just the opposite: he is a figure of capable compassion, a wise man, who goes forth each day in the Chaucerian realization that constantly he must keep appointments that he never made.

What chance has Stephen to distract the reader's interest from so large, so superb a being? Poldy has Shakespearean comedy in his soul; poor Stephen keeps playing an inadequate performance as Hamlet. *A Portrait* is a beautiful and permanent book, but *Ulysses* belongs to the cosmos of the greatest literary art: Chaucer, Shakespeare, Cervantes, Tolstoy, Proust. We give up Stephen because he has been superseded by Leopold Bloom, who touches one of the limits of art. ❁

Biography of
James Joyce

James Joyce appreciated the symbolic importance of his birth date—February 2 in 1882—which fell on Candlemas as well as the day belonging to St. Bridget and the Shadow-seeking Groundhog. His artistry embraced the sublime, the commonplace, and the foolish. "I never met a bore," he earnestly once said and the reader discovers that for Joyce marginal moments in ordinary lives are as likely to carry universal significance as do grand gestures and holy events.

Joyce, the eldest of ten children, was born in Dublin to John Stanilaus Joyce and Mary Jane Murray. The family's declining financial status necessitated several moves but Joyce's childhood recollections included harmonious evenings of singing and conversation with frequent and diverse guests who early introduced him to the controversial issues of faith and politics in Irish life.

John Joyce sent his son at the early age of six and a half to Clongowes Wood College, forty miles from home, to receive a thorough training in traditional and Catholic scholarship from the Jesuits. Although he excelled in his studies and showed some athletic interest, Joyce was not a joiner, and experienced painful episodes of isolation. In one memorable event Joyce's eyeglasses were broken by another student. Believing that Joyce had broken the glasses himself to avoid work, the prefect of studies struck his outstretched hands with a metal and leather stick (a customary punishment called "pandybatting") inflicting pain both corporeal and psychological. With a righteous courage remarkable for his age, Joyce appealed to the school rector. This early experience of being victimized by ignorance and inauthenticity and the subsequent need to seek or even create a higher authority for absolution is a major Joycean theme.

In June of 1891 Joyce was withdrawn from Clongowes for financial reasons. The undistinguished Christian Brothers School was the alternative so Joyce stayed briefly at home. A fortuitous meeting between John Joyce and Father John Conmee, the rector who had believed Joyce's story and recalled his intellectual promise, made it possible for Joyce without fee to attend Belvedere College, the prestigious Jesuit day school.

Contemporary readers discover in Joyce a mix of striking originality and rich traditionalism; features of both began to emerge prominently during his Belvedere years. He studied Latin and French and won prizes for his essays. He pursued his interests beyond the routine assignments. In 1897 he received a prize for the best English composition written by anyone in Ireland in his grade and was known as Belvedere's best scholar. Neighbors from that time recalled him as "grave" and "aloof," but he also enjoyed frivolity, kept up his singing, and occasionally played hooky with his brother Stanislaus. When assigned an essay on his favorite hero, Joyce rejected Achilles and Hector, choosing Ulysses, the wanderer. Other nontraditional heroes appealed to him as well: the once-glorious Lucifer who fell from Paradise for disobeying God; and Charles Stewart Parnell, the beloved would-be Irish liberator whose scandal-ridden fall from fame generated ardent conversations all over Ireland.

When scorned by classmates for defending the Romantic Byron, Joyce fiercely stood alone. When publicly accused of heresy in an essay Joyce retreated by pretending to have meant something else but later reclaimed his position. Both episodes earned for him a reluctant respect among his classmates and foreshadowed the rebellious—even renegade—spirit he became known for.

The adolescent Joyce became disenchanted with his family. He blamed his father for creating chronic crises and troubled his devout and longsuffering mother by refusing to adopt a conventionally pious demeanor. He discovered sensuality with Dublin prostitutes and alternately relished and abhorred his sexual indulgences. He viewed himself as a bestial sinner and was frightened into a period of extreme penance by a school sermon on sin and eternal punishment. Much later, he refused to grant his dying mother's wish that he accept the Church. Joyce's vacillating adherence to Catholic teaching greatly discomfited the priests and fellow Irishmen. A central focus of Joyce's work became the forging of an unfettered artistic sensibility out of the restricting conventions of Irish Catholicism and nationalism.

Joyce entered University College in Dublin in 1898 at the age of sixteen, excelling in everything but chemistry—a failing that rendered unlikely his brief enthusiasm for becoming a doctor. He was a serious and an irreverent student. At graduation Joyce and some companions became unruly at the singing of "God Save the King," which incident brought Joyce to the attention of the police and was the occasion for his spontaneous speech about students having the right to make as much noise as they pleased. He had several writing projects but these survive only in fragments. The important accomplishment of these years was the development of the "epiphany" as a literary device. Joyce described epiphany as a sudden and unbidden moment of memorable clarity revealing a transforming insight. It was the writer's task to record these epiphanies.

Joyce disdained popular expressions of Irish nationalism, and, following a favorable interaction with the writer Ibsen, identified himself as a European and fashioned for himself a kind of exile from Ireland leaving in 1902 to live in Paris. A telegram announcing his mother's illness arrived in April, 1903, and Joyce returned to the family. She died in August. On June 16, 1904 (the day memorialized in *Ulysses*), Joyce began his relationship with Nora Barnacle. Later in the year they left, together but unmarried, to begin a long literary and personal sojourn.

Life in exile—in Trieste, Rome, France, and Zurich—had adventure, frustration, financial insecurity, and, apparently, a great deal of laughter. In a pattern reminiscent of childhood Joyce moved from place to place seeking more comfortable or productive circumstances. But his life also included two children who delighted and astonished him—a son, Giorgio (born 1905) and a daughter, Lucia (born 1907)—as well as a widening circle of friends, admirers, and benefactors. Nora was loyal but Joyce's occasional bouts of drunken carousing worried her.

After nine years of wrangling with publishers Joyce published *The Dubliners* in 1914. *A Portrait of the Artist as a Young Man* attracted Ezra Pound who helped get it published. It appeared in 1916.

Joyce wrote *Ulysses* between 1914 and 1920 and it too was published serially until an obscenity suit was filed against him. The controversy generated additional attention and admiration enabling Joyce to fulfill an earlier wish that he become famous before he died. *Ulysses* was published in 1922 but remained banned in England and America through twelve years of legal battles that ended when Judge Woolsey in the United States exonerated Joyce in 1933. Random House released the book in 1934. The cryptic *Finnegans Wake* was completed in 1939.

Joyce was helped in 1916 by his benefactor Harriet Shaw Weaver, and his own writings began to provide income, but his last years remained difficult. His beloved Lucia was institutionalized with schizophrenia in 1932 and his eyesight, weak since childhood, deteriorated despite eleven operations. Nearly blind and relying on help from others, Joyce died in Zurich on January 13, 1941. He and Nora had married for legal reasons in 1930. She died in 1951, also in Zurich.

No writer since Shakespeare has generated more literary interest and analysis. And *Ulysses,* banned for years, is now read aloud in public places in a widespread recognition of "Bloomsday" every sixteenth day of June. ❀

Plot Summary of
A Portrait of the Artist as a Young Man

During the sixties it became fashionable for young adults who fancied themselves "artistic" to carry in their backpacks a copy of *A Portrait of the Artist as a Young Man*. The novel was not always popular. It was rejected by publishers for being "formless" and full of too many "ugly things." Harry Levin observed in 1941 how short was Joyce's transition from ostracism to canonization. The display of human evil since World War II and the deadening nature of technology reawakened our need for artists to remind us of our ultimate concerns.

The novel's title is important. *Portrait* moves from the earliest experiences of childhood through the emotional upheaval of adolescence to the arrival at young manhood and the emergence of an artistic sensibility that will not end when the novel does. Throughout, we watch the strategies Stephen must both discover and create to make his own way.

On a visit with his father to the anatomy display room of Queen's College, Stephen is startled to find the word "Foetus" carved into a desk. Contemporary readers will need to make an effort to understand the capacity for shock in such a moment. In turn-of-the-century Catholic Dublin, formal restraints on physical, intellectual, or spiritual activity were narrow. The gestating foetus and the emerging embryo of the soul were confined to traditional spaces. The moment in the anatomy room so unnerves Stephen that to compose himself he utters a little chant:

> I am Stephen Dedalus. I am walking beside my Father whose name is Simon Dedalus. We are in Cork, in Ireland. Cork is a city.

Stephen's effort to position himself in the universe is a theme repeated throughout the novel. On the flyleaf of his geography book he has written:

Stephen Dedalus
Class of Elements
Clongowes Wood College
Sallins
County Kildare
Ireland
Europe
The World
The Universe

On the opposite page a school companion has imagined a conventional trajectory for Stephen:

Stephen Dedalus is my name.
Ireland is my nation.
Clongowes is my dwellingplace
And heaven my expectation.

Stephen is one of those children instantly mesmerized by gazing into the starry heavens, but he differs from his contemporaries by speculating about theology and metaphysics—those vexing questions that go beyond reassuringly visible boundaries.

What was after the universe? Nothing. But was
There anything round the universe to show where
It stopped before the nothing place began? . . . It was
Very big to think about everything and everywhere.
Only God could do that . . . It pained him . . . that he did
Not know where the universe ended.

From this uncertain point, Stephen moves on to discover that becoming a true artist will require risk and rebellion resulting in exhilaration but also in pain, isolation, and even greater uncertainty.

Hints of Stephen's artistic inclination appear in **Chapter I**. His first memory is of listening to his father's story about "baby tuckoo." He makes the lines of a song—

O, the wild rose blossoms
On the little green place—

into his own poem—

> O, the green wothe botheth
> [O, the green rose blossoms.]

Wild roses can bloom on a green place, he thinks, but there is no such thing as a green rose. "But perhaps somewhere in the world you could [have a green rose]." "Somewhere" is the human imagination, here, specifically, Stephen's. Earliest impressions are mediated through the five senses: Stephen sees his father's hairy face while listening about the storybook character selling her lemon platt; bed-wetting makes the touch of the sheets first warm and then cold and they have a "queer smell."

Stephen recalls hiding under the table after committing some unspecified misdemeanor. His mother promises that Stephen will apologize but Dante, his righteous caretaker, unleashes a small measure of the fiercely punitive authority Stephen will later encounter. If he doesn't apologize, Dante says, "the eagles will come and pull out his eyes." Both the reader and, apparently, Stephen are ignorant about his error which is precisely the most frightening aspect of punishment.

Chapter I introduces Stephen's earliest memories of being an outsider. This identity takes increasingly grave forms as Stephen grows up. In the midst of schoolboy football, Stephen keeps himself "out of sight of his prefect, . . . feigning to run now and then." This early act of self-exclusion seems connected to Nasty Roche's taunting question: "What kind of a name is that?" Stung and confused, Stephen is reduced to silence. His namesake—Stephen, the first Christian martyr—was stoned by the Jews for reporting a vision. Daedalus was the artist/inventor from classical mythology who fashioned wings for himself to escape imprisonment in a labyrinth. The life-saving impulse to escape confinement will set Stephen apart from his schoolmates, companions, and later, from all his compatriots.

Time is another early theme. Homesick Stephen longs for vacation and counts down the days he has secretly pasted inside his desk. Although helpless to move time to his own advantage, he has a remarkably reassuring perspective on objective time: "Christmas vacation was very far away: but one time it would come because the earth moved round always."

Time also fosters deepening levels of self-awareness. Briefly ill in the school's infirmary, Stephen imagines his death and enjoys the range of emotions and the beauty of the music at his funeral. Out of this pleasantly indulgent reverie, Stephen hears the mundane sounds of the healthy boys at play and ponders the novel thought that the school day is proceeding without him. Despite having no vocabulary to name this insight, Stephen has come upon the possibility of multiple points of consciousness, and therefore of reality—a defining experience for the artist.

The third section of Chapter I contains the extended scene of Christmas dinner. It is 1891; in October Charles Stewart Parnell, formerly exalted champion of Irish nationhood, has died following a year of vilification for adultery. Into the festive family Christmas that Stephen has eagerly anticipated intrudes the controversy. Dante exults in Parnell's downfall which torments John Casey, another guest, and Stephen's father, for whom Parnell is still a beloved figure. The Church joined forces against Parnell. Dante's fierce assertion of God's supremacy brings Mr. Casey out of his chair to denounce God in Ireland. The scene dramatizes Stephen's first exposure to the narrow animosities generated by politics and religion and ends with Stephen's terror-stricken face looking up to find his father in tears.

Another instance of apology and punishment ends the chapter. Back in school Stephen witnesses a student being shamed for an innocent lapse of memory. Father Dolan, on an unannounced visit to catch "lazy idle loafers" accuses Stephen of trickery in pretending his glasses are broken to avoid work, and strikes his hands with a leather and metal strap, the customary punishment known as "pandybatting." Stung by injustice that is worse than the painful humiliation, Stephen appeals to a higher authority in the person of Father Conmee, the rector, who believes him. The oppressive features of early Catholic education are dramatized here but so also is Stephen's choice not to become its victim.

In **Chapter II**, Stephen learns that his father's financial decline will prevent him from returning to Clongowes. For a brief period, Stephen is free on the streets. His likeable uncle Charles, who smokes a noxious tobacco and sings in the outhouse, brings him to chapel but his simple piety leaves his nephew uninspired. Simon encourages his son to be a runner but the trainer's "flabby" face causes Stephen to doubt his father's judgment. Politics do not engage him.

Against this banal backdrop, Stephen reads at night and imagines adventures with himself as hero. He joins a gang of street companions who make pretend-raids on the gardens of old maids.

He is now about fourteen and finishing his second year at Belvedere, the Jesuit day school, where he has been successful as a student, writer, and actor. His isolation, however, continues. The "silly voices" of the children annoy him and he feels himself surrounded by "undistinguished dullards." The earlier playfulness degenerates into the "dull phenomenon of Dublin." A few of the dullards gang up on Stephen when he claims Byron is the greatest poet and Tennyson a mere "rhymester." Heron calls Byron an immoral heretic and demands that Stephen agree. When Stephen hotly refuses, the boys shove him against barbed wire in a scene reminiscent of his beating by Father Dolan. Stephen here becomes a martyr for art. Later he is accused by his Jesuit teacher of writing heresy in an essay, an instance of the Church's attempt to restrict original thought.

Increasingly, Stephen casts aside the oppressive influences. Out with his father and two cronies, Stephen feels "an abyss . . . of temperament sundered him from them." Later he realizes "his childhood was dead . . . and with it his soul capable of simple joys. . . ." There is lament here for something lost. The artist cannot join with others in comfort or strife but rather will elevate their stories with the Aristotelian emotions of pity and terror.

Stephen's emerging sexuality pervades this chapter. For solace and inspiration, the self-isolated Stephen turns to inner experiences and "the company of phantasmal comrades" which comes to include the prostitutes from Dublin's Nighttown. He is fascinated by sin, and following many masturbatory fantasies, craves sinning "with another of his kind. . . ." The chapter closes as Stephen succumbs to his lust and their seductions. He is in "another world" as if "before an altar" in "some rite" that awakens him. The perfumed women in long gowns appear in the gasflames almost like priestesses. Woman idealized as mother and Mary becomes here a prostitute bearing a different kind of knowledge. Joyce's rendering of this forbidden descent into matter and flesh with religious imagery suggests that the artistic sensibility requires an acceptance of all human experience as legitimate material for new creation.

Chapter III begins with Stephen's discovery that all deadly sins arise "from the evil seed of lust." He experiences pride, envy, gluttony, blasphemy, anger, and "the swamp of spiritual and bodily sloth." A consequence of sinning, however, is the emergence of conscience and consciousness. The lustful flesh makes him think anew about the mysterious sacraments of baptism and the Eucharist. If the body of Jesus is in a piece of bread, Stephen ponders, what happens when the bread turns moldy? At a school retreat, he endures a series of prolonged sermons on the four last things of Catholicism: death, judgment, hell, and heaven. With graphic details reminiscent of Dante's *Inferno*, Father Arnall describes the red-hot spikes and suffocating odours in a living hell so convincingly crowded that no one has room to raise an arm to pluck an invading worm out of one's eye. With self-loathing and horror, he learns that he can save himself only by mortifying the very senses that gave him his first impressions of life. He confesses to an unfamiliar priest and is restored to a life of purity.

In **Chapter IV** Stephen enters a joyless discipline. His devout demeanor attracts the attention of a priest at Belvedere who summons Stephen to consider the priesthood as a vocation. But his transformation is uncertain. He asks, "I have amended my life, have I not?" In a pivotal scene Stephen watches the priest coiling and uncoiling the cord from his gown and retreats as if escaping a hangman's noose. Later Stephen realizes that "his destiny was to be elusive of social and religious orders." He would "learn his own wisdom apart from others . . . wandering among the snares of the world" which were its "ways of sin." Joyce's view of this fallen world is not sentimental. Images of disorder and stagnating cabbages follow his resolution.

With lightened heart, Stephen turns toward the sea—eternal resource for ever-renewing life. Here he comes upon a girl wading in the water. The sight brings forth a burst of profane joy. Her perfect image engenders the epiphany Stephen has of his calling to become an artist, joining the Creator of Life to make out of "the sluggish matter of the earth a new . . . imperishable being." Images of soaring and flight bring to focus the significance of Stephen's namesake and his escape from imprisonment. Spent with emotion, Stephen falls into a rapturous sleep.

The ecstasy of Stephen's epiphany cannot be sustained. In **Chapter V** Stephen must confront and overcome other competing influences, represented by his companions, to fully accept his destiny. At the end of *Portrait* Stephen has created and gathered his resources and stands ready to take the risk.

In *Portrait*, chronology is less important than transformative experiences. Stephen moves between extremes that modify without diluting: spirit and matter; time and timelessness; submission and assertion; the sacred and profane. Stephen also carries his early memories through all his experiences to create increasingly rich insights. ❀

List of Characters in
A Portrait of the Artist as a Young Man

Stephen Dedalus is the central figure of *Portrait*. It is his artistic sensibility we watch developing from the earliest childhood experiences of comfort, fear, confusion, and pleasure through the chaotic adolescent emotions associated with sexuality and identity formation up to the discovery of vocation and independence in young adulthood. Stephen's development is especially tumultuous because the influences competing for his allegiance—Irish nationalism and Roman Catholicism—are inimicable to the artistic requirements for originality and authenticity. Stephen's nature is innocent and curious but as he grows he becomes at times arrogant, self-absorbed, and humorless—in short, not always likeable. By the end of the novel Stephen has considered and rejected a calling to the priesthood, discovered his calling as an artist, and is at the point of self-exile from Ireland.

Simon Dedalus is Stephen's decent and well-meaning father. Although he has high regard for his oldest son and makes appropriate efforts to ensure for him the best education, he is incapable of understanding his son's inner turbulence and aspirations. On a trip to his own birthplace in Cork, Simon unknowingly chooses a moment just after Stephen has fallen into a private abyss of adolescent emotions to deliver a little speech encouraging his son to gain a proper status in life for himself by mixing with the "right gentlemen." The father's financial decline is responsible for the frequent moves the family must make.

Uncle Charles is the benignly banal companion for Stephen in his younger years. His tobacco repels and his piety fails to inspire but Stephen finds him accepting and comforting. At the Christmas dinner in Stephen's home Uncle Charles makes an effort to protect Stephen from exposure to the hostility that erupts in the conversation about Charles Stewart Parnell and Ireland's future.

Dante Riordan functions as a caretaker and extended family member in Stephen's household. Her punitive manner and strident religious righteousness create some fearful episodes in Stephen's early years. She speaks the frightening words about the eagles that will tear out Stephen's eyes if he does not apologize.

Father Arnall is Stephen's Latin teacher at Clongowes who confirms to no avail Stephen's story about his broken glasses. Later he delivers the retreat sermon about the punishments of hell which frightens Stephen into a brief period of intense devotion to the Catholic model of purity.

Father Dolan is the prefect of studies at Clongowes Wood College who makes unannounced classroom visits in search of lazy little boys in need of flogging. Father Dolan punishes Stephen unjustly, accusing him of making up his broken glasses story. Stephen appeals to higher authority in the person of **Father Conmee**, rector of the school, who believes his story.

Emma Cleary (E.C.) is the girl who awakens Stephen's romantic life. One of Stephen's artistic accomplishments is a poem inspired by her. At the end of the novel, she seems to find Stephen awkward and difficult to understand.

Cranley, Lynch, Heron, Davin are among Stephen's classmates and companions. Each is associated with some aspect of Stephen's development, particularly with influences Stephen must cast aside. With Cranley Stephen discusses intimate matters; with Lynch he presents theories about art and Aristotelian terror and pity. Heron twice harms him, once as rival for E.C. and again when he strikes Stephen for defending Byron. Davin is the earnest and friendly voice of Irish nationalism. ❀

Critical Views on
A Portrait of the Artist as a Young Man

DEREK ATTRIDGE ON ADVICE FOR FIRST-TIME READERS OF JOYCE

[Derek Attridge received his education in South Africa when the English literary tradition undervalued the works of Joyce. He has since become a prolific Joyce scholar. He edited *The Cambridge Companion to James Joyce* (1990) and has written many books and articles on language and literature. His most recent book is *Joyce Effects: On Language, Theory, and History* (2000). He co-edited *Semicolonial Joyce* (2000). Attridge teaches at the University of York and (as visiting professor of English) Rutgers University. In this extract from the introduction to *The Cambridge Companion to James Joyce*, Attridge acknowledges that the size and variety of critical commentary on Joyce may bewilder new readers looking for help in the library. He offers a framework for approaching Joyce and compelling reasons to do so.]

Reading Joyce's *œuvre* is, as an ever-renewed activity, more than a lifetime's work (or play); and when we take into account the massive heap of books written about that *œuvre* towering around it—and growing larger at an ever-increasing rate—the task of even beginning to feel at home with Joyce may make the newcomer quail. But there is no need for alarm: none of those books is essential to the reader of Joyce in search of pleasure and understanding, and at the same time all of them are potential allies. ⟨. . .⟩ Take the library shelves which hold a hundred books containing interpretations of Joyce: they also hold, inside those same books, much of Joyce's text itself, quoted, paraphrased, fragmented, dispersed, rearranged, expanded. In reading through those books you are reading, and rereading, the Joycean text itself, seen from constantly-changing viewpoints and enhanced by ever new juxtapositions.

However, there is no need to move beyond the original work at all to experience its special rewards. Help in reading Joyce is not confined to the books that surround his own; his texts themselves teach us how to read them, provoking laughter at our *naïveté* when we fall into the trap of thinking of the world they create as a world that existed before they brought it into being, encouraging us to do without our need for singleness of meaning or certainty of position, showing us how our language is a powerful, and powerfully funny, determiner—but also underminer—of our thoughts and acts. Many of the most influential literary theorists of the past twenty years, whose views have percolated into thousands of classrooms, have testified to the importance of reading Joyce in the development of their ideas.

So Joyce's work has actually been growing over the years, and the number of ways of reading it has also been growing, all of them of some value, none of them final or definitive. There could not possibly be a 'correct' way of reading, or even starting to read, the textual mass that consists of Joyce's texts themselves, all the texts of which *they* are readings, ⟨. . .⟩ all the works of Joycean criticism and biography which read *them,* all the transcripts and facsimiles of manuscript material, and all the other texts which have a potential bearing on Joyce. ⟨. . .⟩

The number of entrances to the Joycean mansion, therefore, is potentially infinite; the main requisites for a visit are a sharp eye and ear, a willingness to be surprised, and of course a sense of humour.

—Derek Attridge, ed., *The Cambridge Companion to James Joyce* (New York: Cambridge University Press, 1990): pp. 23–24, 28.

HERBERT S. GORMAN ON *PORTRAIT* AS OBJECTIVE AUTOBIOGRAPHY

[Herbert S. Gorman (1893–1954) was a novelist and an influential literary critic. Among his publications are *Hawthorne: A Study in Solitude* (1927) and *A Victorian American: Henry Wadsworth Longfellow* (1926). In the following extract, taken from *James Joyce: His First Forty Years* (1926), Gorman explores the autobiographical nature of *A Portrait of the Artist* and the power with which Joyce reveals Stephen Dedalus's inner life.]

"A Portrait of the Artist as a Young Man," of course, is autobiography. Indeed, the progress of Joyce's mind since *Dubliners* has been almost wholly autobiographical. Most of the time he is concerned with himself and his reactions to environment. The emphasis is on spiritual environment. With this for his subject-matter Joyce set out with his new technique and delivered himself of a novel that is mainly subjective but which is starred with the most distinguished objective pictures. They story is one of the boyhood and youth of Stephen Dedalus, an Irishman brought up and educated by Jesuits. Stephen is sensitive, brooding, and delicately cerebrated. Upon the clear slate of his consciousness, his environment draws dark and forbidding lines. His boyhood is unusual insomuch as it is an unending stream of personal reactions to even the lightest touches of the existence into which he has been flung. The unique qualities of the novel are to be found in the revelation of the youth's unspoken thoughts, the setting down of the sometimes unconscious stream with a cold candor and deliberate frankness that was not to be found in the fiction of its day. There is a Rousseau-like self-flagellation in some of this material. We cannot doubt that. Joyce is turning himself inside out, spilling forth all the jangled moods that lie deep in artistic consciousness. The sensibilities of Stephen Dedalus are evidenced in such magnificent chapters as the religious retreat where the horrors of Hell are pictured by a priest and before whom the boy grovels in the intense fanatic-grip of his faith, in the long talk with Lynch in which Stephen outlines his aesthetic theories, and in the last beautiful chapters where Stephen, now almost a man, passes through the white, torturing fire of his love-affair simultaneously with the realization that he has lost his faith.

In essence, the book describes a formal, tawdry environment crushing a spirit that was born to be free, a spirit that will fight back and follow the flame, which it sees dancing before it. Stephen knows that he is being crushed by a physical and intellectual leanness, that the props beneath him are rotten. As we witness the Dedalus family disintegrating throughout the pages of "A Portrait of the Artist as a Young Man" we observe, at the same time, the result of his gradual sinking in the muck on the sensitive mind of the young man. What progress can there be in a life like this for him? The gradual knowledge comes to him that he must leave it, that he must exile himself from it and long before those final pages when he eventually does prepare to leave Ireland it is quite perceptible that Stephen is an exile ⟨. . .⟩ There are times when Joyce writes impartially but we feel that behind these impartial sentences there is a far from impartial man. In order to write so he must lift the scourge to his own back. Roman Catholicism is in his bones, in the beat of his blood, in the folds of his brain and he cannot rest until it is either removed or clarified. It is his misfortune that it may never be removed. It will pervert his nature but it is there, twisted out of all resemblance to itself even in the frankest passages. The vivid, highly-functioning mind of the Stephen Dedalus of "Portrait of the Artist as a Young Man" is the mind of a Mediæval Catholic. If the same mind had been twisted to the other side of the line, it would have been to the intense visioning of a religiast.

—Herbert S. Gorman, *James Joyce: His First Forty Years* (London: Geoffrey Bles, 1926), pp. 72–74, 75.

HARRY LEVIN ON STEPHEN AS ARTIST

[Harry Levin (1912–1994) was the Irving Babbitt Professor of Comparative Literature at Harvard University. He published extensively on literature and modern languages. In this extract, taken from *James Joyce: A Critical Introduction* (1941), Levin looks at some of the interior features and pre-occupations of an artistic sensibility.]

Stephen is ever susceptible to the magic of names—particularly of his own last name. Names and words, copybook phrases and schoolboy slang, echoes and jingles, speeches and sermons float through his mind and enrich the restricted realism of the context. His own name is the wedge by which symbolism enters the book. One day he penetrates its secret. Brooding on the prefect of studies, who made him repeat the unfamiliar syllables of "Dedalus," he tells himself that it is a better name than Dolan. He hears it shouted across the surf by some friends in swimming, and the strangeness of the sound is for him a prophecy: "Now, at the name of the fabulous artificer, he seemed to hear the noise of dim waves and to see a winged form flying above the waves and slowly climbing the air. What did it mean? Was it a quaint device opening a page of some medieval book of prophecies and symbols, a hawklike man flying sunward above the sea, a prophecy of the end he had been born to serve and had been following through the mists of childhood and boyhood, a symbol of the artist forging anew in his workshop out of the sluggish matter of the earth a new soaring impalpable imperishable being?"

⟨. . .⟩ The richness of his inner experience is continually played off against the grim reality of his external surroundings. He is trying "to build a breakwater of order and elegance against the sordid tide of life without him."

⟨. . .⟩ At school, he takes an equivocal position, "a free boy, a leader afraid of his own authority, proud and sensitive and suspicious, battling against the squalor of his life and against the riot of his mind." At home, he feels "his own futile isolation." He feels that he is scarcely of the same blood as his mother and brother and sister, but stands to them "rather in the mystical kinship of fosterage, foster child and foster brother."

Joyce's prose is the register of this intellectual and emotional cleavage. ⟨. . .⟩

⟨Discussing his esthetic ideas with the dean of studies, Stephen attaches a cluster of literary associations with sense impressions of the moment, creating a state of mind that⟩ exalts the habit of verbal association into a principle for the arrangement of experience. You gain power over a thing by naming it; you become master of a situation by putting it into words. It is psychological need, and not hyperfastidious taste, that goads the writer on to search for the *mot juste,* to loot the thesaurus. Stephen, in the more explicit manuscript, finds a treasurehouse in Skeat's *Etymological Dictionary.* The crucial moment of the book, which leads to the revelation of his name and calling, is a moment he tries to make his own by drawing forth a phrase of his treasure:

> —A day of dappled seaborne clouds.—
> The phrase and the day and the scene harmonised in a chord. Words. Was it their colours? He allowed them to glow and fade, hue after hue: sunrise gold, the russet and green of apple orchards, azure of waves, the greyfringed

fleece of clouds. No, it was not their colours: it was the poise and balance of the period itself. Did he then love the rhythmic rise and fall of words better than their associations of legend and colour? Or was it that, being as weak of sight as he was shy of mind, he drew less pleasure from the reflection of the glowing sensible world through the prism of a language manycoloured and richly storied than from the contemplation of an inner world of individual emotions mirrored perfectly in a lucid supple periodic prose.

—Harry Levin, *James Joyce: A Critical Introduction* (Norfolk, Conn.: New Directions, 1941): pp. 46, 48–49, 50–51.

JAMES T. FARRELL ON THE BURDEN OF IRISH HISTORY IN JOYCE'S WORK

[James T. Farrell (1904–1979) was an American novelist and an important literary critic and reviewer. His works include *A Note on Literary Criticism* (1937) and *Literary Essays, 1954–1974* (1976). In the following extract, taken from *The League of Frightened Philistines and Other Papers* (1945), Farrell compares Stephen's attempts to escape the paralysis of his Irish background to Joyce's own stylistic and literal exile from Ireland.]

What Stephen sees is Irish history in the present, in terms of what has happened to Ireland and to Irishmen as a result of their defeats. But Stephen does not dwell on a tragic past in moods of regret. Rather, he is bitter because of the condition of the Ireland he knows, the Ireland inherited from a tragic historic past. During the period when he was still at work on *A Portrait of the Artist as a Young Man*, Joyce, in a letter, describes Dublin as a "center of paralysis." It should be realized that it was Joyce who introduced the city realistically into modern Irish writing. The city—Dublin—is the focus of Ireland in his work, and in his life. We see that this is the case with Stephen, the genius son of a declassed family. Stephen lives, grows up in a Dublin that is a center of paralysis. Is he to have a future in such a center? Is he to prevent himself from suffering paralysis, spiritual paralysis? Stephen's painful burden of reality can be interpreted as a reality that derives from a history of Ireland's defeats and that is focused, concretized, in the very quality of the men of Dublin. Stephen describes his own father to a friend as "A medical student, an oarsman, a tenor, an amateur actor, a shouting politician, a small landlord, a small investor, a drinker, a good fellow, a storyteller, somebody's secretary, something in a distillery, a tax gatherer, a bankrupt, and at present a praiser of his own past." Just as Stephen says he has been produced by "This race and this country and this life," so can this be said of his father. It is in this way, and in the image of his own father that we can realize how Stephen carries a sense of Ireland's history in his own consciousness. And at the same time he feels that he is a foreigner in Dublin, a foreigner in the sense that he is even forced to speak a language not his own. Just before his discussion of esthetics with the Jesuit dean of studies, Stephen realizes that "The Ireland of Tone and of Parnell seemed to have receded in space." He, Stephen, living in the Ireland after their failure, thinks, while talking to the dean: "I cannot speak or write these words without unrest of spirit. His language [the dean's], so familiar and so foreign, will always be for me an acquired speech. I have not made or accepted its words. My voice holds them at bay. My soul frets in the shadow of his language." Stephen's thoughts are highly suggestive, highly important, for an interpretation of this novel. When Joyce walked the streets of Dublin as a youth, one can be sure he constantly sensed the presence of the English in the major city of Ireland. One can speculate by asking how many little incidents, words, gestures, angers, glances of suspicion did he not grasp on the wing, all deepening a sense of the life of Dublin as a painful burden? The failure of the Irish to follow men like Tone and Parnell, meant that he, Stephen, must fret in speaking a language not his own. Again, it is revealed how Irish history presses on Stephen as something concrete, immediate, as a condition of life that affects him, threatens him with paralysis of soul. Such being the case, it should be clear as to why Joyce could find no inspiration in a cultural renaissance that found so much of theme and subject in a legendary Irish past. A real Irish presence was far, far too disturbing. Herein is the meaning of a remark Stephen utters in his own defense: "I am not responsible for the past." But, to repeat, he has seen the consequences of that past all about him in the present.

And since this is the case, Joyce is not going to find literary inspiration where the leading literary men of the time found it. He does not have to discover Ireland. He carries too much of it already in his own being.

—James T. Farrell, "Joyce's *A Portrait of the Artist as a Young Man,*" (1944; reprinted in *The League of Frightened Philistines and Other Papers,* New York: Vanguard, 1945), pp. 49–51.

WILLIAM YORK TINDALL ON THE ESCAPE THEME

[William York Tindall (1903–1981) taught *Ulysses* to his classes at Columbia University while the book was still banned. The school's single (and bootlegged) copy was chained to the library where Tindall's students went to read their assignments. He wrote thirteen books on British authors including four on Joyce. In this extract, taken from *A Reader's Guide to James Joyce,* Tindall discusses the competing claims on Stephen's soul and the different features of the artist's need to escape them.]

Escape has three aspects: negative or getting away from an intolerable situation; positive, for freedom to create; and romantic or a kind of Byronic expansiveness and exploratory enlargement. Stephen, an impatient romantic and potential creator, is moved by all three. Fascinated with words, as a man of letters must be, he finds the necessity for escape in a series of terrible verbs, all imperative in mood: *apologize, admit, submit, obey, confess, commune, conform.* The eagle of authority, threatening his eyes unless he apologize, shows all these imperatives forth. Indeed, that demanding bird with his hypnotic rhyme first appears in Joyce's little book of epiphanies. Heron's "admit," supported by cane and cabbage stump, is the second of these radiant imperatives for Byronic Stephen, a proclaimed "heretic," and later an "out-law." "Obey," "confess," and "commune" are the burden of the retreat in the school chapel; and "conform," though unspoken, is implicit in the final interview with Cranly. As for "submit," like Mr. Browne of *Dubliners,* it is everywhere.

These imperatives are the "nets" which the outlawed heretic and self-proclaimed creator must fly above in order to find the "unfettered freedom" that creation demands. In exile, with a creator's cunning, "I will try to express myself," he says, "in some mode of life or art as freely as I can and as wholly as I can." As Cranly observes, the penalty of escape, whether positive, negative, or romantic, is loneliness, not only man's general condition in our time, if we believe Conrad, Kafka, and many others, but a particular improvement on it: "Alone, quite alone. . . . And you know what that word means? Not only to be separate from all others but to have not even one friend." It may be, as John Donne affirms, that no man is an island, but the daring young man wants to be one and leave his. ⟨. . .⟩

In any case, his first attempt at exile is unsuccessful. The first chapter of *Ulysses* shows him back in Ireland, still silent, with cunning unimpaired. At the end of *Ulysses* he tries again, more successfully maybe, though we never know. If for the moment we may confuse Stephen's undisclosed but implied future with Joyce's past, Stephen is to remain obsessed with what he has rejected. He only thinks he has given up being lover of the place he is lover of. Physically abroad, he never leaves home; for exile fails to diminish his concern with Ireland and her traditions. Indeed, coming to terms with Ireland (at a distance) seems to be Stephen-Joyce's success. Though this success is implicit in *Ulysses,* it is altogether absent in *A Portrait,* which ends with the artist's beginning.

—William York Tindall, *A Reader's Guide to James Joyce* (New York: Octagon Books, 1959): pp. 57–59.

RICHARD ELLMANN ON EXILE AS ARTISTIC FREEDOM

[Richard Ellmann (1918–1987) the renowned biographer and literary critic, lectured at Harvard University, Yale University, the University of Oxford, and the University of Chicago. He is the author of *Yeats: The Man and the Masks* (1948), *The Identity of Yeats* (1954), and *Oscar Wilde* (1987). His monumental work, *James Joyce* (1959), changed the way many scholars viewed the art of biography. In the following extract, Ellman comments on exile and artistic freedom in *A Portrait of the Artist.*]

Revolutionaries fatten on opposition but grow thin and pale when treated with indulgence. Joyce's ostracism from Dublin lacked, as he was well aware, the moral decisiveness of Dante's exile from Florence in that Joyce kept the keys to the gate. He was neither bidden to leave nor forbidden to return, and he did in fact go back four times. But whenever his relations with his native land seemed in danger of improving, he found a new incident to solidify his intransigence and reaffirm the rightness of his voluntary exile. He even showed some grand resentment at the possibility of Irish independence on the grounds that it would change the relationship he had so carefully established between himself and his country. "Should I," he asked someone, "wish to alter the conditions that have made me what I am?" At first he thought only his soul was in danger in Ireland. Then, when his difficulties over the publication of *Dubliners* became so great, he thought his writing career was being deliberately conspired against. Finally he came to assert that he was physically in danger. This suspicion began when his wife paid a visit to Galway in 1922. Civil war had just broken out in the west, and her train was fired on by soldiers. Joyce chose to believe that the bullets were really aimed at him, and afterwards refused to return to Ireland because he said he feared for his life. That Joyce could not have written his books in Ireland is likely enough, but he felt the need for maintaining his intimacy with his country by continually renewing the quarrel with her which prompted his first departure.

In his books too his heroes are outcasts in one way or another, and much of their interest lies in why they are cast out and by whom. Are they "self-doomed," as Joyce says of himself in his broadside, "The Holy Office," or are they doomed by society? To the extent that the hero is himself responsible, he is Faust-like, struggling like Stephen Dedalus or Richard Rowan to achieve a freedom beyond human power. To the extent that society is responsible he is Christ-like, a sacrificial victim whose sufferings torment his tormentors. Joyce was not so masochistic as to identify completely with the helpless victim; at the very moment he attacks society most bitterly as his oppressor, he will not completely deny the authorship of his own despair. Like the boy in the ballad of the Jew's daughter, he is immolated, *consenting*. Again he was not so possessed with self as to adopt utterly the part of the anarchic individual. He carefully avoids making his heroes anything but unhappy in their triumphant self-righteousness.

Half-willing and half-forced to be a sufferer, Stephen endows the artist in *A Portrait of the Artist as a Young Man* with a rather similar mixture of qualities, the total power of a god bored by his own handiwork and the heroic impotence of a Lucifer, smarting from pain which he has chosen to bear. To be both god and devil is perhaps to be man. In *Ulysses* the paradoxes ascribed to these forces are the paradoxes of being Joyce: God begets Himself, sends himself between Himself and others, is put upon by His own friends. Joyce and Stephen challenge in the same way the forces which they have brought into being. As Stephen says of Shakespeare, "His unremitting intellect is the hornmad Iago ceaselessly willing that the moor in him shall suffer." If the residents of heaven were not androgynous, he says, God would be bawd and cuckold too, arranging for his own humiliation with his own creatures.

In his books Joyce represents heroes who seek freedom, which is also exile, voluntarily and by compulsion. The question of ultimate responsibility is raised and then dropped without an answer. Joyce's hero is as lonely as Byron's; consequently Joyce obliterated Stephen's brother, Maurice, from the *Portrait* after using him tentatively in *Stephen Hero,* for there must be no adherent, and the home must be a rallying-point of betrayal.

A cluster of themes—the sacrilege of Faust, the suffering of Christ, the exile of Dante—reach a focus in the problem of friendship. For if friendship exists, it impugns the quality of exile and lonely heroism. If the world is not altogether hostile, we may forgive it for having mistreated us, and so be forced into the false position of warriors without adversaries. Joyce allows his hero to sample friendship before discovering its flaws, and then with the theme of broken friendship represents his hero's broken ties with Ireland and the world.

—Richard Ellman, "A Portrait of the Artist as Friend," *The Kenyon Review* 18, no. 1 (Winter 1956): pp. 53–55.

[Deborah Pope teaches English at Duke University. She wrote *Ties That Bind: Essays on Mothering and Patriarchy* (1990) and *Fanatic Heart* (1992) and is currently co-editing a series on pedagogy and gender. In this extract, Pope observes Joyce's mingling of sacred and profane references in the descriptions of Stephen's most formative experiences. Joyce's belief that sacred and profane knowledge were overlapping and not distinct was one of the ways he distanced himself from the prevailing Roman Catholic culture in Ireland.]

Joyce commonly uses the language of spirituality and conventional theology to expand and redirect the nature of the emotional intensity occasioned by a secular epiphany. For example, Stephen's initial encounter with the prostitute and his later trembling submission to communion generate identical feelings of response, the irony of which goes unrecognized by him. In turn, his religious epiphanies are consistently turned to secular uses. Thus, the masochistic series of physical and sensual mortifications he deliberately undergoes in a burst of fervid religiosity only serve to subtilize and extend the very senses they are designed to subdue. Rather than accentuate the ascetic, they further Stephen's apprenticeship as an artist. The interpenetrability of the religious and secular clearly broadens the thematic level and resonance of particular passages thus connected. The two sections detailing Stephen's personal visions of hell—his lurid hallucination following the retreat sermon—and of heaven—his beatific encounter with the bird-girl—exemplify such a linkage. ⟨. . .⟩

Stephen's metaphoric descent into hell, like his ascent into an aesthetic heaven, is private, uniquely vouchsafed him by a higher power. Roused by the retreat sermon to intensities of fear and self-revulsion, he is driven to extravagantly hallucinate out of his surfeited sense of guilt. Escaping to his room, he is reluctant to cross the threshold, dreading what reproach or terror awaits. ⟨. . .⟩ A similar, though muted, sensation of fear comes over Stephen along the seawall: "A faint click of his heart, a faint throb in his throat told him once more of how his flesh dreaded the cold infrahuman odour of the sea ⟨. . .⟩.

Not the least of the parallels is the surprising resemblance of landscape, first evident in the curious quality of light and foulish air:

A faint marshlight struggled upwards from all the ordure through the bristling greygreen weeds. An evil smell, faint and foul as the light, curled upwards sluggishly out of the canisters. . . . A rictus of cruel malignity lit up greyly their old bony faces. ⟨. . .⟩

He was alone . . . amid a waste of wild air and brackish waters and the seaharvest of shells and tangle of veiled grey sunlight.⟨. . .⟩

When Stephen cries out, "Help!" as the goats move, and "Heavenly God!" as the girl stirs, in a sense the cries are reversed. More appropriately speaking, it is a "Heavenly God" whom the hell-vision affirms, while it is a truer "help" that the mortal beauty affords him. The prayer Stephen utters after the goatish hell is, in effect, a plea the wading girl answers. In that early fervent address to the Virgin, she is the figure *"with a creature's comeliness and lustre suited to our state,"* whose *"very face and form, dear mother, speak to us of the Eternal . . . telling of Heaven and infusing peace."* Through this invocation, the figure of Mary is introduced into the vision, offering redemption, as her counterpart on the sea-strand similarly offers Stephen new life. Yet, through the scrupulous repetition of "hither and thither," even to the number of times it occurs, Joyce has undeniably linked the girl with the goats as well. What happens is that the symbolic function of the goats divides: their importance for aesthetic development, and as indicators of natural, ineradicable drives, is taken over by the girl, while their more exaggerated representation of Stephen's still ambivalent sexual maturity is taken over by the scampering boys. The girl on the strand, that marvelous compaction of the promptings of Stephen's ways and days, is beautifully, ironically, in one supreme stroke, both Virgin and goat. She is indeed the reconciling angel of life, the apotheosis of carnal and spiritual, here for the first time in Stephen's mind in graceful balance.

—Deborah Pope, "The Misprision of Vision: 'A Portrait of the Artist as a Young Man,' *James Joyce Quarterly* 3, Vol. 17 (Spring 1980).

[Suzette Henke teaches in the Department of English at Ohio Wesleyan University. She wrote *The James Joyce Songbook*, a collection of two hundred songs important to Joyce. Her purpose was to give readers a sense of what music meant for Joyce's imagination and how specific songs are used in *Ulysses*. In this extract, from *Women in Joyce*, which she co-edited, Henke discusses Stephen's relation to women in a Freudian context.]

In a confused way, Stephen tries to fathom the mysteries of Oedipal attraction. He is unable to differentiate between filial and erotic love and feels perplexed when Wells unites the two in a sexual conundrum: "Tell us, Dedalus, do you kiss your mother before you go to bed?" ⟨. . .⟩ As the curious child stumbles toward manhood, he feels compelled to cast off allegiance to maternal figures. His childhood educator Dante, "a clever woman and a wellread woman" who teaches him geography and lunar lore, is supplanted by male instructors: "Father Arnall knew more than Dante because he was a priest." The Jesuit masters invite Stephen to ponder the mysteries of religion, death, canker, and cancer. They introduce him to a system of male authority and discipline, to a pedagogical regiment that will insure his "correct training" and proper socialization. Through examinations that pit red rose against white, Yorks against Lancastrians, they make education an aggressive game of stimulated warfare. The students, like soldiers, are depersonalized through institutional surveillance. ⟨. . .⟩

When Stephen again returns to Clongowes, he realizes that his mother cannot offer a viable sanctuary from the male-dominated power structure that controls the outer world. He must learn to survive in a society that protects bullies like Wells and sadists like Father Dolan, that condones brutality, and that takes advantage of the weak and the helpless. The pandybat incident at the end of chapter 1 symbolically reinforces the rites of objectification characteristic of Jesuit training. Father Dolan's authority is absolute and unquestioned. He relies on patriarchal privilege and assumes a "panoptical" vision: "Father Dolan will be in to see you every day." Branded as "lazy little schemer," Stephen must endure the ignominy of being misnamed and robbed of subjective identity.

The young boy is being socialized into what Philip Slater identifies as a culture of male narcissism. According to Slater, single-sex education and the separation of male children from the emotional refuge of the family promotes misogyny, narcissism, and a terror of the female. Boy children suffer from an "unconscious fear of being feminine, which leads to 'protest masculinity,' exaggeration of the difference between men and women." Once the child is deprived of maternal affection, he "seeks compensation through self-aggrandizement—renouncing love for admiration—and in this he is encouraged by the achievement pressure placed upon him, and presumably by the myriad narcissistic role models he finds around him. He becomes vain, hypersensitive, invidious, ambitious, . . . boastful, and exhibitionistic."

Stephen's appeal to Father Conmee is motivated not only by optimistic faith in a male-controlled world, but by personal vanity and a tendency toward exhibitionism. His youthful vision is blurred, idealistic, and Panglossian. He naively believes that he will be exonerated simply by presenting his case before a higher patriarch. In his confrontation with the rector, Stephen makes a symbolic rite of passage through the primordial chambers of racial and ecclesiastical history. He asserts his budding manhood against totalitarian power and is acclaimed a revolutionary hero by "the Senate and the Roman people." But the triumphant child later discovers the aftermath of his rebellion: Dolan and Conmee, in smug condescension, "had a famous laugh together over it." Stephen has unwittingly played the ingenuous fool at the court of his Jesuit masters. In a bold attempt to assert masculine independence, he has served merely as an object of paternal amusement.

—Suzette Henke, ed., *Women in Joyce* (Urbana, Chicago, London: University of Illinois Press, 1982): pp. 82–91.

[Don Gifford taught English at Williams College. He wrote
Notes for Joyce: Dubliners *and* A Portrait of the Artist as a
Young Man (1967) and *Notes for Joyce:* Ulysses (1974). Gifford
is one of those gifted scholars of Joyce who make his work
more accessible for readers. His books contain encyclopedic
references and can be used as guides. In this extract, Gifford
puts the famous sermon in a context that illuminates Joyce's
purpose and enables the reader to more keenly appreciate the
sermon's impact on Stephen's young and vulnerable mind.]

The retreat at Belvedere College which provides the narrative structure of this chapter is organized on the model of *The Spiritual Exercises* (1548) of St. Ignatius of Loyola. *The Exercises* suggest four
weeks of meditation on: (1) sin and its consequences (Hell); (2)
Christ's life on earth; (3) Christ's Passion; and (4) His risen life. The
fictional Father Arnall's sermons concentrate heavily on week (1),
with some attention to week (2). St. Ignatius in part provides for this
in paragraph 4 of the *Exercises*:

> Although four weeks are assigned . . . nevertheless this is
> not to be understood, as if each week necessarily contained
> seven or eight days. For since it happens that in the First
> Week some are slower than others in finding what they
> desire, namely, contrition, grief and tears for their sins; and
> likewise some are more diligent than others, and more agi-
> tated or tried by different spirits, it is sometimes necessary
> to shorten the Week, at other times to lengthen it . . .

But while *The Spiritual Exercises* underpin the narrative structure,
the specific patterns of Father Arnall's sermons, together with their
language, are derived from a devotional text, *Hell Opened to Chris-
tians, To Caution Them from Entering into It,* written in 1688 by the
Italian Jesuit, Giovanni Pietro Pinamonti, translated anonymously
(Dublin, 1868). Joyce borrowed extensively from Pinamonti,
rewriting and tailoring his text to the dramatic situation of the
novel. James R. Thrane has extensively demonstrated the nature and
scope of Joyce's use of Pinamonti. The following notes to chapter III
make no attempt at a thorough coverage of Joyce's use of this source
since such coverage, while it would provide an interesting case study
of Joyce's methods of composition, would not contribute directly

to a reader's understanding of Father Arnall's sermons within the larger patterns of the novel. It should be noted, however, as Thrane has pointed out, that there was an intense controversy on the subject of eternal damnation in the late nineteenth century, particularly among Protestant theologians, many of whom condemned as unthinkable cruelty the doctrine of eternal punishment without hope. The Catholic response to this controversy was guarded but also divided between "liberals" and "dogmatists" or "rigorists." Joyce's sermonological versions of Pinamonti's meditations (and their impact on Stephen) are clearly intended as a dramatic instance of the psychic impact of the dogmatist or rigorist point of view. One commentator, Father Noon, acknowledges the sermons' "dramatic effectiveness in context" but at the same time objects: "The purely negative and harrowing sermon of the *Portrait* is neither Catholic nor Ignatian." The objection is instructive since it suggests that Joyce's purpose was not necessarily to be Catholic and representative but to outline one of the opposing points of view in a public controversy and to dramatize its impact on an impressionable mind.

Pinamonti's meditations are divided into two groups: I. on *poena sensus* (the sensory pain suffered by the damned), A. The Prison of Hell, B. The Fire, C. The Company of the Damned; and II. on *poena damni* (the pain that stems from the eternal loss of the beatific vision), A. The Pain of Loss, B. Remorse of Conscience, C. The Pain of Execution, D. Eternity. Father Arnall's sermons follow this general pattern.

—Don Gifford, *Joyce Annotated: Notes for* Dubliners *and* A Portrait of the Artist as a Young Man (Berkeley and Los Angeles, Calif.: University of California Press, 1982): pp. 177–78.

RICHARD F. PETERSON ON READER'S VIEWS ABOUT STEPHEN

[Richard Peterson teaches English at Southern Illinois University. He writes frequently on Irish literary figures. He is currently working on *James Joyce: A New Look*. This extract is taken from *Works in Progress: Joyce Centenary Essays* (1983) which he co-edited.]

The key to the criticism of *A Portrait of the Artist as a Young Man* has been the personality of Stephen Dedalus and Joyce's own attitude or distance from that personality. While the title clearly claims a special genius for Stephen—that of the artist—and modifies that genius by fixing it at a stage of potential or development—as a young man— critics have often chosen between "the artist" or "the young man" in their judgment of Joyce's intention in the novel.

Those who read the novel as a portrait of artistic genius usually sympathize with Stephen's ordeals, approve his aesthetic theory as Joyce's own, and see him triumphing over his treacherous environment by flying into a self-imposed exile to write a masterpiece. Others, influenced by Hugh Kenner, find only a young man in the novel and condemn Stephen's actions, mock his aesthetics as juvenile, and judge him as a case of arrested development in spite of Stephen's talk about creating the uncreated conscience of his race. Kenner has been especially vigilant and aggressive in deprecating Stephen, describing him as a fake artist, "indigestibly Byronic," and most recently as the spiritual brother of the broken or resigned failures in *Dubliners*.

This debate over Stephen's personality and whether or not he will ever write the works of genius of his creator has obviously influenced the study of the narrative form of *A Portrait*. Stephen sympathizers plunge into an impressionistic flux and see that flux forming itself into a process of becoming out of which Stephen finally emerges as the artist-creator of his own life. Stephen haters remain aloof from the narrative itself and find the novel an ironic demonstration of the failure of talent or genius to express itself except in "rebellious bohemianism." They judge Stephen a hopeless product of his environment, his generation, and his own sensibility.

While the debate continues between critics who argue for an impressionistic narrative of becoming and those who see an ironic narrative demonstrating a finished state, some have perceived a double vision forming the narrative. This view takes into account what appears to be both artistic involvement and detachment within the novel. Unfortunately, since the emphasis here is on vision, or how Joyce perceives his own novel, those who see both Joycean compassion and irony have trouble deciding whether Joyce's portrait is one of compassionate irony or ironic compassion. In other words, that same enigma, the virtues and vices of Stephen's personality, also haunts those who see someone to admire and to dislike, but cannot decide where to place the emphasis.

—Peterson, Cohn, Epstein, eds., *Works in Progress: Joyce Centenary Essays* (Carbondale and Edwardsville: Southern Illinois University Press, 1983): pp. 15–16.

Joseph A. Buttigieg on Stephen's Obstacles to Becoming an Artist

[Joseph A. Buttigieg is a Joyce scholar and author of *A Portrait of the Artist in Different Perspective*, from which the following extract is taken. Buttigieg compares Stephen's attempt to escape history with the necessity of developing new critical approaches to Joyce's work.]

Stephen Dedalus recognizes early in his life the need to escape the murderous burden placed upon him by a sacrosanct tradition. In both *A Portrait of the Artist as a Young Man* and *Ulysses* we find him struggling against the nets which constrain him and the ghosts that haunt him. In both novels, Joyce traces the progress of Stephen as he moves wilfully toward fulfilling his self-imposed artistic vocation. Yet, it must be stressed, Joyce never produces a picture of Stephen as creator but only of Stephen in the throes of becoming a creator. Whatever Stephen might think of himself, there should be little doubt that in *A Portrait* and in *Ulysses* he is still struggling against those forces which prevent him from attaining the status of a genuine, as opposed to a self-styled, artist. The forces which campaign against Stephen's emergence as artist, in the full Nietzschean sense of creator, are the ghosts of history, the phantasms of his own past as well as the phantasms foisted upon him by his country and his religion. The two are hardly separable. Stephen is not unaware of these ghosts nor is he blind to their pervasive influence. He knows he has to free himself from the excess of history in order to become the creator of a new order; "—History, Stephen said, is a nightmare from which I am trying to awake." Nevertheless, Stephen often fails to realize fully the extent to which he is enmeshed in that nightmare, and consequently his declarations of freedom are, with possibly one exception, premature. (The possible exception occurs when Stephen smashes the lamp with his ashplant in the phantasmagoric "Circe" chapter [of *Ulysses*].) There is one thing, however, which Stephen thoroughly understands and about which he is certain: in order to escape paralysis he must "bring the past to the bar of judgement, interrogate it remorselessly, and finally condemn it."

In our time, the conflict with the inherited tradition in literary critical studies must likewise take the form of a remorseless interrogation which should result in a *critical* (in the Nietzschean sense) history of Modernism. The classics of Modernism present the postmodern age with a problem not entirely different from the one which for Pope and Dryden was posed by the Greek and Roman classics—they threaten to become a debilitating force, they might induce paralysis. Hence, one of the most pressing needs of postmodernism is to produce a critical history, as opposed to a monumental history, of Modernism. The postmodern age must construct its own definition of Modernism. In a sense, of course, Modernism has already been defined and its monuments identified; but the prevailing definitions of Modernism and the privilege conferred upon certain texts deemed central to it come to us as part of that very same tradition which we must now confront critically and "interrogate remorselessly." For this reason, the construction of a postmodern definition of Modernism is inseparable from the "destruction" of the received tradition. "Destruction" here derives its special meaning from Martin Heidegger who, like Nietzsche, has made clear the problem that arises from the uncritical acceptance and transmission of tradition. "When tradition thus becomes master, it does so in such a way that what it 'transmits' is made so inaccessible, proximally and for the most part, that it rather becomes concealed. Tradition takes what has come down to us and delivers it over to self-evidence; it blocks our access to those primordial 'sources' from which the categories and concepts handed down to us have been in part quite genuinely drawn. Indeed it makes us forget that they have had such an origin. . . ." To overcome this forgetfulness Heidegger proposes the critical method of "destruction." As he hastens to make clear, "to bury the past in nullity . . . is not the purpose of this destruction; its aim is *positive*." Destruction enables the interpreter "to go back to the Past in a positive manner and make it productively his own." ⟨. . .⟩

The importance of Joyce's texts in the Modernist pantheon is so great that any attempt to understand Modernism must include a careful consideration of Joyce's novels and the preeminent—one might even say paradigmatic or classic—status they enjoy. Yet, precisely because these texts are constitutive of Modernism as it has been habitually understood, it is especially difficult to examine them anew. They cannot be separated easily from the tradition which they both exemplify and constitute. It is quite hard to read them in a manner that differs significantly from the way in which they have already been read and presented. Still, any new beginning with regard to these texts must contend with the problem of extricating them from the authoritative critical and historical literary discourse that envelops them. In other words, if Joyce's *A Portrait of the Artist as a Young Man* and *Ulysses* are to be reappropriated for a postmodern readership, if they are not to be abandoned as the beautiful but ossified monuments of a dead past (i.e., a Modernism that once was and is no more), then their reappropriation will involve an analysis and critique of Modernism. Simultaneously, a critical or revisionary approach to Modernism necessarily entails a reconsideration of its canonical texts among which Joyce's novels occupy a very special place. These two tasks are one and the same and must be carried out concurrently because they cannot be separated effectively.

—Joseph A Buttigieg, *A Portrait of the Artist in Different Perspective* (Athens: Ohio University Press, 1987), pp. 10–12.

KAREN LAWRENCE ON JOYCE'S VIEW ABOUT WOMAN

[Karen Lawrence has written on feminism in Woolf, Charlotte Brontë, and Joyce. She wrote *The Odyssey of Style in "Ulysses"* (1981) and edited *Transcultural Joyce* (1998). She is currently editing *Canonical Reconsiderations of Twentieth-Century British Literature*. Literary feminists have recently focused attention on Joyce. In this extract, taken from her essay "Joyce and Feminism" in *The Cambridge Companion to James Joyce,* Lawrence asserts that women exist in Joyce's writing mainly as enablers of male development.]

In the early portraits of the artist, *Stephen Hero* and *A Portrait,* women seem to be once again cast in roles auxiliary to male development—as sexual tutors (the prostitute), muses (E.C., the bird girl), and symbols of the entangling snares the developing male must avoid (temptress of the villanelle, E.C., Dante with her hysterical Catholicism). The development of the Daedalean artist seems to entail a flight from women, particularly the mother, as a condition of growth. She is one of the 'nets' he must fly by. In order to enter the symbolic world of language and the Father, the boy must remove himself from 'the sufferings of women, the weakness of their bodies and souls'. ⟨...⟩

It is as if the image of the female were abstracted by Joyce so that Stephen must incarnate it himself, for ultimately Stephen seeks to convert abstract beauty and desire into poetry. As he has his 'epiphany' of the bird girl at the end of part IV, Stephen feels 'her image pass into his soul for ever'. But he begins to realize that the image must pass out as well, if he is to be a 'priest of the eternal imagination' and transmute the spirit into a material image. The muse is crucial to this incarnation; somehow it is her spirit that must be embodied. One might say with Molly that all poets merely 'want to write about some woman', but the female is more than a topic here; she is projected as the muse of representation, of embodiment. Her image haunts his days and his nights, as he struggles to refine it into poetry.

In part V Stephen seeks to find an image for E.C., between temptress and muse, inspiration for a wet dream and for poetry. In the process of figuring her, the young artist hopes to capture her elusive power, yet, he questions his own images, disturbed that he cannot fully represent her. He tries first one, then another image, crossing out as he goes along, debating how to figure her in language. ⟨...⟩

The maternal image, too, seems beyond Stephen's control, surfacing at a crucial moment like the return of the repressed. The moment occurs in *A Portrait* during Stephen's trip to Cork, his father's hometown, when he searches for his father's initials in a school desk. Instead, in the midst of his search for his paternal origins, he is startled to find the word 'foetus', carved in the desk like a scar. As Maud Ellmann says in a brilliant discussion of this episode, Stephen, searching for his father's (and thus his own) initials, discovers instead an image that draws him back to the body of the mother. In the midst of the scripting of the artist in the patriarchal tradition, the word leads back to 'a prior nameless unbegotten world'. The mother's anonymity flouts the name of the father. ⟨. . .⟩

—Karen Lawrence, "Joyce and Feminism." In *The Cambridge Companion to James Joyce*, Derek Attridge, ed. (New York: Cambridge University Press, 1990): pp. 246–248.

JOHN PAUL RIQUELME ON OSCILLATIONS IN STYLE AND NARRATIVE

[John Paul Riquelme teaches at Southern Methodist University in Dallas, Texas. He is currently working on a new study of T. S. Eliot. In this extract, taken from *The Cambridge Companion to James Joyce,* Riquelme discusses the practice in *Portrait* of Blake's idea ("Without Contraries is no progression") as a device Joyce used to enhance the meaning and method of Stephen's development.]

The results of that practice emerge ⟨. . .⟩ when the alternation tending toward a process of extremes merging and mutually modifying one another becomes an important structural principle in Joyce's subsequent writing. By using styles that often work by means of oppositions in order to present a character whose thoughts and experiences regularly involve opposing forces, Joyce enables readers to recognize a variety of possible resemblances and differences between the writer and the character. The same language pertains simultaneously, though in different ways, to the writer who has learned to work successfully with contrasts and to the character whose life is filled with them. ⟨. . .⟩

⟨. . .⟩ By alternating and starkly juxtaposing extremes, Joyce arranges the events of Stephen's life without relying primarily on continuity of action. ⟨. . .⟩ *A Portrait* is episodic, ⟨. . .⟩ ⟨Joyce abandons⟩ narrative continuity in order to make moments that are separated in time contiguous in the narration.

Even within the individual, juxtaposed moments of elevated climatic insight and countering, realistic perception, a pattern of contrast and possible merger sometimes appears. When this happens, a highly complex process of reading can ensue that may be understood to mimic Stephen's process of recollection. The possibilities for this kind of reading emerge most emphatically late in the narrative, once the reader has come to know Stephen's thinking, especially the language of his thinking, well. It would seem that Stephen remembers at some level his earlier experiences, which have become connected with one another and tend at times to merge. The situation is complicated because he apparently remembers and connects elevated moments of insight not just as a group but in some relation to the moments of realistic perception that always follow them. And he remembers and combines other experiences as well. Joyce does not present Stephen explicitly remembering and linking the opposing moments. He depends instead on the reader's remembering, connecting, and anticipating. And he presents Stephen's thoughts in language that, by repeating aspects of earlier scenes, suggests that a remembering and crossing-over may be taking place.

A kind of feedback is created whereby Stephen's later experiences, which are in some ways repetitions of earlier ones, are not in fact exact repetitions, in part because they occur against the background of what has gone before. The reader has access to this feedback through the increasingly mixed language that leads back to earlier scenes of different kinds. Because the language is complexly layered, the reader comes to every scene with frames of reference derived from earlier elements of the narrative, but each scene in turn results in new retrospective framings of what has gone before and new prospective framings of what is to come, and so on until the various frames overlap or nest within one another. The highly unusual effect, which is difficult to describe in an expository way, mimics the process of Stephen's remembering his complicated, differential past as he encounters each new experience, but it depends on the reader's active recollection of earlier passages.

—John Paul Riquelme, In *The Cambridge Companion to James Joyce,* Derek Attridge, ed. (New York: Cambridge University Press, 1990): pp. 117–118.

[John Blades is the author of *James Joyce: A Portrait of the Artist as a Young Man* (1991), from which the following extract is taken. Blades explores Joyce's definition of "epiphany" as both a revelation of truth and a "heightened spiritual elation."]

Fundamental to an appreciation of Joyce's approach in *A Portrait* is an understanding of his concept of the "epiphany" and its use. As defined by Stephen and used by Joyce, it is crucially important not only to this novel but to all of Joyce's work, since in its implications it widely embraces the themes of time, truth, morality and art. However, *A Portrait* marks a step forward for Joyce's development as a writer in that, while all his previous work—*Chamber Music, Dubliners,* and *Stephen Hero*—also employs essentially isolated epiphanies held together in varying degrees of unity, *A Portrait* incorporates a sequence of related epiphanies in the form of a coherent narrative.

⟨. . .⟩ What exactly does Joyce mean by the word? For a formal definition of "epiphany" we must go outside *A Portrait* and to its earlier version, *Stephen Hero,* where Stephen, idly composing his "Villanelle of the Temptress" in Chapter XXV, overhears fragments of a conversation between two people:

> This triviality made him think of collecting many such moments together in a book of epiphanies. By an epiphany he meant a sudden spiritual manifestation, whether in the vulgarity of speech or of gesture or in a memorable phase of the mind itself. He believed that it was for the man of letters to record these epiphanies with extreme care, seeing that they themselves are the most delicate and evanescent of moments. He told Cranly that the clock of the Ballast Office was capable of an epiphany. Cranly questioned the inscrutable dial of the Ballast Office with his no less inscrutable countenance.
> —Yes, said Stephen. I will pass it time after time, allude to it, refer to it, catch a glimpse of it. It is only an item in the catalogue of Dublin's street furniture. Then all at once I see it and I know at once what it is: epiphany.
> —What?

> —Imagine my glimpses at that clock as the gropings of a
> spiritual eye which seeks to adjust its vision to an exact
> focus. The moment the focus is reached the object is
> epiphanized.

Joyce, of course, borrows the term from the religious context—the
feast day celebrating the revelation of the infant Christ to ordinary
mortal mankind represented in the three Magi. Clearly, Joyce's
concept takes up this idea of a manifestation—a showing forth of
the reality of an object, a person, an event, etc. to the observer, with
the suggestion also of privileged spiritual insight. Joyce discovered
the phenomenon early in his teens, and Stanislaus [Joyce] in his
biography records his brother's practice of collecting such
moments:

> . . . manifestations or revelations . . . little errors and ges-
> tures—mere straws in the wind—by which people betrayed
> the very things they were most careful to conceal. "Epipha-
> nies" were always brief sketches . . . (*My Brother's Keeper*)

In *Chamber Music,* almost every poem is centred on a single precise
epiphany, presented with youthful reverence, while in *Dubliners,*
each story consists of one or a number of epiphanies by which a
character (and/or the reader) comes to realize the truth of his circumstances and the paralysing limitations of them. On the other
hand, in *Ulysses,* an older, self-mocking Stephen scorns his own
youthful reverence for epiphanies and his eager collecting of them,
as he contemplates his languishing artistic ambitions:

> Remember your epiphanies written on green oval leaves,
> deeply deep, copies to be sent if you died to all the great
> libraries of the world, including Alexandria? Someone was
> to read them there after a few thousand years . . .

In *A Portrait,* Joyce advances the use of epiphanies not only as a fundamentally significant literary technique but also as an important
philosophical concept which was to become the cornerstone of his
own mature works—and a cornerstone of Modernism in general.

In Stephen's definition and in Joyce's practice the term has two
meanings: one is that an epiphany reveals the truth, the intrinsic
essence of a person or of something which is observed, revealed perhaps through a "vulgarity of speech or of gesture"; and the second

meaning is a state of mind, heightened spiritual elation of the observer's mind, what Joyce calls the "memorable phase of the mind itself." The first puts emphasis on the object and the fact that its reality can be revealed by an epiphany, while the second puts emphasis on the observer, for whom an epiphany can be a state of spiritual ecstasy. Consequently, although we would normally think of the acquisition of knowledge in terms of a rational process, both of these meanings involve non-rational states, and insofar as they involve knowledge (either about an object or about oneself), the process implies a subjective source of truth, knowledge as a sort of intuition. In fact, as Stanislaus records, epiphanies can even include dreams—especially so since Joyce considered dreams to be a subconscious reshaping or sharpening of everyday reality.

—John Blades, *James Joyce: A Portrait of the Artist as a Young Man* (London: Penguin Books, 1991): pp. 155–157.

JEAN-MICHEL RABATE ON JOYCE'S VIEW OF THE PERSONALITY OF THE WRITER IN THE TEXT

[Jean-Michel Rabate is a French literary critic currently teaching at the University of Pennsylvania in Philadelphia. In this extract, taken from *James Joyce Authorized Reader* (1991), Rabate looks at the first words uttered by Stephen without intercession by the narrator.]

Joyce, it is true, does not say that the author has died, preoccupied as he is with dead mothers and dying fathers, but states that he has been "refined out of existence": "The personality of the artist, at first a cry or a cadence or a mood and then a fluid and lambent narrative, finally refines itself out of existence, impersonalises itself, so to speak. . . . The artist, like the God of the creation, remains within or behind or beyond or above his handiwork, invisible, refined out of existence, indifferent, paring his fingernails." This well-known passage finds its source in Flaubert's letters about the impersonality of the writer. ⟨. . .⟩ The theory is hardly one entailing a diminished role: the godlike artist disappears tactically; he is not absent but just hidden, and his famous "indifference" is not that of Pascal's *Deus absconditus* but that of a *Deus larvatus,* all the more present because of his invisibility. ⟨. . .⟩

This role is reserved to Stephen Dedalus, Joyce's "altar ego," on the opening page of *A Portrait of the Artist as a Young Man,* as the reader is given a clue of Stephen's budding vocation when Stephen's voice is heard for the first time:

> *O, the wild rose blossoms*
> *On the little green place.*
> He sang that song. That was his song.
> *O, the green wothe botheth.*

With the distortion of "O the green rose blossoms," baby Stephen conflates the two lines of the song "Lily Dale," thereby positing his first creative gesture, enabling him to really "possess" or own "his" song: he creates a green rose, an ideal rose that bypasses the traditional opposition between a white and a red rose: "White roses and red roses: those were beautiful colours to think of. . . . Lavender and cream and pink roses were beautiful to think of. Perhaps a wild rose might be like those colours and he remembered the song about the wild rose blossoms on the little green place. But you could not have a green rose. But perhaps somewhere in the world you could." The green rose constitutes Stephen's Irish answer to the dilemma set up as a trap by the Jesuits: either York or Lancaster. In so doing, he forges an impossibility, which cannot exist "in the world," but only in language. Such a language is, of course, Anglo-Irish, an Anglo-Irish itself predetermined by another opposition between maroon and velvet. However, Stephen's green rose is not necessarily a proof of his identification with Parnell's green leaf; it is not yet an "ivy leaf." The key to the distortion of the song is the pun: Stephen distorts "blossoms" into "botheth," which should suggest a verbal form based on "both." His refusal to choose between antagonistic colors becomes a verb implying growth and the fusion of the contraries. "Bothing" is a "wild" action, generating a luxuriant and overabundant linguistic procreation, both "in" the world, and more romantically, "anywhere out of the world." A first instance of Stephen's creative mistakes, the "green rose" embodies the linguistic process underlying *Finnegans Wake.*

Thus the process of "forging" cannot be limited to the subjective sphere of the budding artist; on the other hand, Stephen must be made to acknowledge himself as an artist ⟨. . .⟩ so that the reader can be shown the way towards self-authorization. ⟨. . .⟩

—Jean-Michel Rabate, *James Joyce Authorized Reader* (Baltimore, Maryland: Johns Hopkins University Press, 1991): pp. 3, 6–7.

JOSEPH CAMPBELL ON MYTHIC AND HEROIC ASSOCIATION WITH STEPHEN

[Joseph Campbell (1904–1987), author of *Hero of a Thousand Faces* (1949, rev. 1980) and *Myths to Live By* (1972), is widely known for his studies of folklore and myth. This extract is from *Mythic Worlds, Modern Words: On the Art of James Joyce* (1993).]

> O, the wild rose blossoms
> On the little green place.

Already we have mythological images: the little green place and the wild rose blooming. The rose is the mandala, the symbol of the center towards which we are going to move, and it is already connected in the youngster's mind to the little green place: a little plot of land, but also Ireland. By centering this Ireland image in the cosmic image, Joyce addresses the problem I spoke of earlier: the transition from a provincial, limited experience of religion, race, and loyalties to a larger archetypal understanding. ⟨. . .⟩

Some time later, Stephen goes to Cork with his father and sees him joshing with his old friends. By this point, Stephen feels quite dissociated from his father. He is beginning to know something; he is growing up; he is learning. ⟨. . .⟩

> Stephen watched the three glasses being raised from the counter as his father and his two cronies drank to the memory of their past. An abyss of fortune or of temperament sundered him from them. His mind seemed older than theirs: it shone coldly on their strifes and happiness and regrets like a moon upon a younger earth.

Here we have a whole train of fundamental images. The main motif is the moon, a worldwide mythological image. The moon dies and is resurrected every month. It carries its own shadow in itself, in contrast to the sun, which is luminous and radiant and scatters shadows before it. ⟨. . .⟩

He has not experienced the orthodox sentiments of childhood and young manhood. What do you do when you don't experience orthodox sentiments? Can you go on accepting the world that lives by them? He is already in exile. Remember: Stephen is still just a boy in school. ⟨. . .⟩

⟨After Stephen has been invited to consider the priesthood as his vocation, he⟩ thinks about priests who condemn books they haven't read and about how they talk in clichés. The images of the tradition are being communicated by people who have not had equivalent affect experiences; there is a dissociation of image from affect. Stephen, who takes the vow of vocation very seriously to his heart, is aware of this split, of the priests not being what they stand for, so he does not know what path to follow. He wants not just to fall into a job, but to determine what his life is going to be. ⟨. . .⟩

⟨After Stephen states his intention to leave the church, and⟩ his friend presses, asking if Stephen fears Judgment Day and everlasting hell-fire, Stephen makes this terrific statement:

> I do not fear to be alone or to be spurned for another or to leave whatever I have to leave. And I am not afraid to make a mistake, even a great mistake, a lifelong mistake and perhaps as long as eternity too.

That is to say, I may burn in hell for this—and this is courage: the courage of facing complete shipwreck on the rocks, disaster, schizophrenic disintegration, hell, anything.

—Joseph Campbell, *Mythic Worlds, Modern Words: On the Art of James Joyce* (New York: Harper Collins, Publishers, Inc., 1993): pp. 32, 35–37, 43, 48.

Jacques Mailhos on Remembering Thoughts in Connection with Places

[Jacques Mailhos teaches translation and English literature at the University of Orleans. This extract is taken from his essay, "The Art of Memory: Joyce and Perec," which appears in *Transcultural Joyce* (1998).]

⟨I⟩n *A Portrait of the Artist*, we see how Stephen builds his memory loci on the model of the map of Dublin:

> In the beginning he contented himself with circling timidly around the neighbouring square or, at most, going half way down one of the side streets: but *when he had made a skeleton map of the city in his mind* he followed boldly one of its central lines until he reached the custom house.

We see here first Stephen's need to memorize the map of the city before being able to wander in it (as he does in *Ulysses*) but also, and most of all, the true construction of memory loci in his mind. Indeed, the mnemonic use of this "skeleton map" which he has thus built (or imagined) for himself clearly appears at the beginning of part V:

> The rainladen trees of the avenue evoked in him, as always, memories of the girls and women in the plays of Gerhart Hauptmann; and the memory of their pale sorrows and the fragrance falling from the wet branches mingled in a mood of quiet joy. His morning walk across the city had begun, and *he foreknew* that *as he passed* the sloblands of Fairview *he would think of* the cloistral silverveined prose of Newman, that *as he walked along* the North Strand Road, glancing idly at the windows of the provision shops, *he would recall* the dark humour of Guido Cavalcanti and smile, that *as he went by* Baird's stonecutting works in Talbot Place the spirit of Ibsen would blow through him like a keen wind, a spirit of wayward boyish beauty, and that *passing* a grimy marineleader's shop beyond the Liffey *he would repeat* the song by Ben Jonson . . . (my emphasis)

Here indeed, we clearly see the Dublin topology of the dedalian memory begin to structure itself, while there also appears the possibility of its functioning on the mode of the narrative journey or trajectory, as will be the case in *Ulysses* (see for example the "Wandering Rocks" chapter). What is important in this passage is the gradual transition between a fairly common type of associative memory (which, to schematize, could be termed Proustian), with a beautiful chiasm linking the "fragrance" of "the rainladen trees" with "the memory of the pale sorrows of the girls and women in the plays of Gerhart Hauptmann," to a more systematic development of the use of the "skeleton map of the city" as a mnemonic scheme, which is clearly marked in the text by the use of the verb "to foreknow" (indicating that Stephen's "morning walk across the city" need not necessarily be real for all the images to be revived) as well as by the use of the modal "would," which might almost be interpreted here in its frequentative sense.

This is the type of "experiment" to which Quintilian refers in his presentation of the art of memory:

> This achievement of Simonides appears to have given rise to the observation that it is an assistance to the memory if places are stamped upon the mind, which anyone can believe from experiment. For when we return to a place after a considerable absence, we not merely recognise the place itself, but remember things that we did there, and recall the persons whom we met and even the unuttered thoughts which passed through our minds when we were there before. Thus, as in most cases, art originates from experiment.
>
> —Jacques Mailhos, "The Art of Memory: Joyce, and Perec." In *Transcultural Joyce,* Karen Lawrence, ed. (Cambridge: Cambridge University Press, 1998): pp. 154–155.

[Here Derek Attridge returns the reader to an earlier stage of life when words carry additional power when they are incompletely understood. He connects this phenomenon of language with young Stephen's unusual responsiveness to words. The extract is taken from *Joyce Effects: On Language, Theory, and History*.]

> Suck was a queer word. The fellow called Simon Moonan that name because Simon Moonan used to tie the prefect's false sleeves behind his back and the prefect used to let on to be angry. But the sound was ugly. Once he had washed his hands in the lavatory of the Wicklow Hotel and his father pulled the stopper up by the chain after and the dirty water went down through the hole in the basin. And when it had all gone down slowly the hole in the basin had made a sound like that: suck. Only louder. ⟨. . .⟩

Although Stephen's vigorous response cannot be explained in terms of inherent aesthetic and onomatopoeic qualities, we can find other reasons for it, reasons not consciously available to the six-year-old boy but still operative upon him. In particular, the word, as used in this schoolyard scene, evokes a realm of taboo sexuality, a realm of which Stephen would be slowly becoming aware in the schoolboy milieu of Clongowes Wood College, with the usual mixture of excitement, ignorance, guilt, and fantasy.

⟨. . .⟩ How is it that language can produce physical sexual effects, as it seems to in Stephen, even though at this early age he has no sexual vocabulary by means of which to describe his reaction? And how is it that language, in the form of literary writing, can produce a similar effect upon the reader—if not an actual physical response, at least an intensity and immediacy of reaction which comes close to physical sensation? Readers of *A Portrait* have frequently found these paragraphs, like the rest of the opening pages of the novel, remarkably vivid, and it seems likely that this vividness stems from more than just the accurate evocation of a young boy's attempts to understand language and its relation to the world he is also trying to come to terms with. That is to say, something rings true, in the mind, in the body, about Stephen's false linguistic theorizing: Joyce makes it possible for the reader to share his protagonist's experience of a word's peculiar intensity and physicality when uttered in a certain context. The early reviews of *A Portrait* testify to the shock of an encounter with language that has an unwontedly direct effect, often combined with a sense of disgust that is itself perhaps testimony to the immediacy of the feelings and sensations conveyed. The following are a few snippets, which could be multiplied at great length, all from 1917 reviews: 'an astonishingly powerful and extraordinarily dirty study . . . absolutely true to life—but what a life!' (*Everyman*); 'My Joyce has a cloacal obsession . . . by far the most living and convincing picture that exists of an Irish Catholic upbringing' (H. G. Wells, *Nation*); 'like the unwilled intensity of dreams' (A. Clutton-Brock, *Times Literary Supplement*); 'brutal probing of the depths of uncleanness' (*Literary World and Reader*); 'What he sees he can reproduce in words with a precision as rare as it is subtle . . . Mr Joyce plunges and drags his readers after him into the slime of foul sewers' (*Freeman's Journal*). We are less likely to be disgusted today, and perhaps the intensity of our reaction is to that degree dulled, but many readers continue to report that intensity and precision of physical and mental evocation is what draws them repeatedly back to *A Portrait,* and particularly to its opening chapter. ⟨. . .⟩

—Derek Attridge, *Joyce Effects: On Language, Theory, and History* (Cambridge: Cambridge University Press, 2000): pp. 60–61, 64–65.

Thematic and Structural Analysis of *Ulysses*

First-time readers of *Ulysses* will be heartened to know that the novel—formidable as it is in length, complexity, and depth—is an engaging and memorable book. One is astonished by Joyce's innovations and networks of meaning. Often—with many critics ready to explain why—the reader just laughs out-loud. Joyce himself acknowledged the difficulty but his readers, in increasing numbers, register their devotion by engaging in marathon readings of the novel, pilgrimages to Dublin streets, and other whimsical rituals in a worldwide celebration of "Bloomsday" every sixteenth of June.

The 768 pages of *Ulysses* cover the activities of one day in Dublin as experienced by hundreds of citizens including, most prominently, Stephen Dedalus and Leopold and Molly Bloom. The date—June l6, 1904—appears once randomly in the novel, but the day is importantly associated with the relationship of Joyce and his wife, Nora. In each chapter, Joyce creates different arrangements of reality so that Dublin life is not seen from one dominant viewpoint. Throughout, members of Dublin's diverse population wander in and out of the narrative presenting fragments of their stories that sometimes make sense and sometimes dissolve into puzzles or just disappear. Lots of scholarly time has been spent examining the cornucopia of details, adding impressively to our enjoyment and understanding, but Joyce's remark that his novel was about everything would give the chronic human experience of feeling puzzled a legitimate place.

Beneath the entangling connections are simple and universal patterns: Bloom has breakfast in the morning, leaves the house to engage in activities for sustenance, pleasure, and duty, then returns home; Stephen, a young man, seeks his place in the world; and Molly stays home.

Joyce initially provided an overall plan for the novel by linking the eighteen chapters with episodes from Homer's *Odyssey*. Outlines of Homeric parallels are easily available; the most extensive is Stuart Gilbert's study, *James Joyce's* Ulysses (1930). Correspondences exist between most chapters and an organ of the body, a time of day, a style of writing, and some category of human activity.

In *The Republic* Plato shows the souls of dead people choosing their next life and describes Odysseus, weary from his tumultuous wanderings, deciding to return as a person of no obvious importance. Joyce never mentions this reference, but he read widely and probably knew it. The question for many readers is whether the Homeric parallels—Bloom as a modern Odysseus, Stephen as Telemachus the son, and Molly as Penelope, awaiting her husband's return—enhance the value of these Dubliners' lives or reduce them through contrast with classical heroic qualities. Or—to ask it differently—was Joyce being ironic? Joyce removed the references to Homeric parallels in the final printing of the book, but it remains customary to use them as organizing principles.

Ulysses is divided into three parts: the Telemachiad (the son's dilemma), the Odyssey (going home), and the Nostos (about return). The first three chapters on Stephen link *Portrait* with *Ulysses*.

Chapter I—"Telemachus"

Stephen's day begins in the old Martello tower overlooking the Bay of Dublin. He has returned from Paris (anticipated at the end of *Portrait*) to attend to his dying mother. With no new plan to escape Dublin, he shares living space with Buck Mulligan, medical student, and Haines, the Englishman. It is eight in the morning. Before anyone leaves for the day two important themes are introduced. The irreverent Mulligan taunts Stephen about his refusal to kneel at his mother's bedside flooding Stephen with sadness and guilt. The presence in memory of the dead mother and the absence of the living father who cannot provide stability to the remaining family members leave Stephen adrift. The tower, built to deter the Irish rebellion, recalls his disenchantment with Ireland's diminished stature; Haine's condescending interest in Irish folklore amplifies his disaffection. Like the Hamlet he broods on, Stephen is at odds with his life.

Chapter II—"Nestor"

At ten in the morning Stephen is teaching history at Mr. Deasy's school to boys neither bright nor interested. A poem about Lycidas who died by drowning but assured of resurrection sets Stephen to brooding again on his mother's death—a part of his own history he wants to escape. The chapter contains Stephen's famous remark, "History is a nightmare from which I am trying to awake," which occurs in an exchange with Mr. Deasy who believes that history is God's manifested will. Stephen resists Ireland's suffering as an act of divine justice. He calls God "a shout in the street"and holds Him responsible for the nightmare. The submissive and bigoted Mr. Deasy is only thinly reminiscent of the kindly advice-giver who encourages Telemachus, but he reminds Stephen that "To learn, one must be humble." Stephen takes his paycheck and promises to deliver a letter on hoof-and-mouth disease to the editor of the newspaper.

Chapter III—"Proteus"

Stephen sets off for Sandymount Strand in the late morning. He sits by the sea, which, being depth itself, gives access to his depths. His interior monologue reveals the quality and depth of his estrangements—both metaphysical and practical. The Sea-God Proteus, representing instability in the physical world, set the seas in chaotic motion to confuse Odysseus. Menelaus, seeking direction for Telemachus, succeeds in getting word of his father's whereabouts. Stephen needs direction and a way to give form to life, which seems meaningless in its ceaseless ebb and flow. This is the calling of the artist: to give form to chaos; in Stephen's case, to write. And he does write, tearing off a piece of Mr. Deasy's letter to record his thoughts. He also expresses his first identification with Irish suffering, acknowledging that the blood of the famine-stricken Irish runs in him, too. This Stephen is less arrogant. He is genuinely lost and knows it. He decides to leave the tower because Haines frightens and Mulligan scorns him. Now literally homeless, he also decides to leave his only income-producing job with Mr. Deasy.

Chapter IV—"Calypso"

Part Two covers the time frame Stephen has just passed through. Leopold Bloom is at home at 7 Eccles Street, preparing breakfast for his wife, Molly, still upstairs in bed. The reader learns that he eats animal organs, has sensual fantasies, is devoted to Molly and disturbed to notice her concealing a letter from Blazes Boylan who writes to announce a visit to deliver the program for her upcoming concert. Bloom suspects adultery, broods on it all day, and will turn out to be right. He reads a sweet letter from daughter Milly and is reminded of son Rudy who died as an infant. References are made to his Jewish roots but he carries in his pocket as a charm an ancient Irish potato. In an exchange with his cat, he wonders how he looks from her perspective (maybe a tower?) and how it feels to be a mouse. Bloom can imagine other points of view. Like Stephen he has an unorthodox relation to his religion (he eats pork, Stephen won't pray) and both are keyless for the day—locked out of their homes. Stephen muses on the beach about change and identity; Bloom explains metempsychosis to Molly. Calypso detained Odysseus for seven years. The parallel is inexact. Bloom sees nymphs everywhere, but Molly is at once Calypso who detains him by distraction, and Penelope, to whom he returns.

Chapter V—"The Lotus-Eaters"

Odysseus' men ate the narcotic lotus flower and became lethargic and forgetful of duty. At ten in the morning Bloom leaves for work but succumbs early to a fantasy correspondence between himself as Henry Flower, Esq. and a Martha Clifford—a lonely strategy to avoid the problems of being Molly's husband. Seeking a discreet place to read his letter, Bloom enters a church while the Eucharist is being enacted. He thinks of religion as one of the opiates to lull pain and earlier observed that a soldier's uniform diminishes his personal responsibility for war. Flowers, perfume, and drugs fill the chapter. Bloom orders lotion for Molly and buys lemon-scented soap for himself. Anticipating the luxury of lying naked in the bath, he thinks of the Eucharist and says: "This is my body."

Chapter VI—"Hades"

This chapter about death reveals Bloom's social isolation. He enters a carriage taking mourners to the funeral of Paddy Dignam in Glasnevin Cemetery, passing on the way statues of Ireland's famous dead and slaughter-bound cattle. Bloom's companions are less friends than acquaintances, and Bloom is excluded in numerous subtle ways. Asking "Are we all here now?" Martin Cunningham then makes room for Bloom. On the way Blazes Boylan is spotted and discussed while Bloom stares down at his fingernails. A sighting of Stephen and talk of suicide bring Rudy's death and Bloom's father to mind, leaving him without connection to his own lineage. An anti-Semitic comment about a money-lending Dubliner awkwardly excludes Bloom. At the gravesite, Bloom, uncomforted by the unfamiliar ritual, speculates alone about grisly and poignant matters: decomposition, rats, and the possibility of being buried alive. He says to himself: "If we were all suddenly somebody else." But his endearing wit is intact: he invents a scheme to put a telephone into the coffin in case the inhabitant wants out, and he muses about Paddy, who, even though dead, beats them all to the cemetery. Odysseus visited Hades in the Underworld and emerged with information and a renewed sense of life; Bloom leaving the cemetery thinks: "Plenty to see and hear and feel yet."

Chapter VII—"Aeolus"

Homer's Aeolus ties the wind into windbags to help Odysseus get home but the crew unties the bags and all is again adrift. The chapter takes place in the office of the "Freeman's Journal and National Press" and is full of the long-winded hot air of newspaper rhetoric. Bloom, a freelance ad canvasser, arriving to arrange an advertisement for Keyes, the spirits merchant, and Stephen with Mr. Deasy's letter intersect for the first time. Both continue to be outsiders. Bloom is mostly ignored and Stephen is offered a job inconsistent with his artistic sensibility. The chapter marks a departure in Joyce's style from the mix of narrative and interior monologue to one appropriate to the setting—varieties of journalistic rhetoric. Stephen offers his "Parable of the Plums," an alternative to overblown political posturing. The chapter ends with Stephen offering to buy drinks for the older men and Bloom feeling compassion for this appealing and vulnerable youth.

Chapter VIII—"The Lestrygonians"

Nearly everyone is eating in this chapter, including Bloom who leaves Burton's restaurant repelled by the sight of greasy men wolfing down their sloppy food. It is one in the afternoon and Bloom, still hungry, goes to Davy Bryne's pub. On the way Bloom responds empathetically to a report of Mina Purefoy, who has been in labor for three days. He feeds the gulls and expresses sympathy for animals awaiting slaughter, although he is not a vegetarian. Stopping to help a blind man cross the street, Bloom reveals again his compassionate nature as well as a subtle morality when he wonders—thinking from the man's point of view—exactly how to be helpful without appearing condescending. Wondering why God permits such apparently undeserved suffering—speculation that links him to Stephen—he humbly concludes he does not understand divine justice. He suddenly fears that Boylan might have a venereal disease. Later he succumbs to a memory of himself and Molly in happier times that contrasts with his present frustration. He is again watching with dread the approaching hour of Boylan's visit to Molly. Many of Odysseus' men were eaten by the cannibalistic Lestrygonians who, in this chapter, are reincarnated in Burton's restaurant from which Bloom flees in disgust rather than fear.

Chapter IX—"Scylla and Charybdis"

At two in the afternoon Stephen is at the National Library with contemporary literary figures and a few companions. Asked about his *Hamlet* theory Stephen gives an abstruse response about the relation of father to son to ghost. In the banter that follows Mulligan mocks, Haines misunderstands, and most of the others are not interested in his idea. Stephen is again injured by his isolation but briefly crosses paths with Bloom on an unrelated errand that sets up a significant interaction for them later in the evening. Mulligan, seeing Bloom, calls him "the Wandering Jew" and, without reason, warns Stephen against him. Stephen resolves to end his relationship with Mulligan.

Chapter X—"The Wandering Rocks"

The City of Dublin is both location and subject. Midpoint in the novel and the afternoon an unorganized procession of citizens beginning with Father Conmee and ending with the cavalcade of the Right Honorable William Humble displays for the reader the range of loyalties and identities available to the next generation of Dubliners. In nineteen sections of varying lengths people walk here and there with simple, absent, or inscrutable purposes. There are random sightings—a dentist named Bloom unrelated to Leopold, and telling juxtapositions—Bloom and Boylan separately buy gifts for Molly, and Stephen and Bloom stand at separate bookstalls. Stephen feels compassion for his sister, Milly, who appears nearly destitute, but gives her none of his money. Bloom (the reader learns) has given generously to the fund for Paddy's son. Molly throws a coin to the one-legged sailor that Father Conmee has just passed not so generously. There are no wandering rocks in Homer's *Odyssey*. Odysseus bypasses them but in this chapter there is both wandering and colliding.

Chapter XI—"The Sirens"

The Sirens are temptresses who lure sailors to their death with enchanting songs. In Chapter XI Bloom faces his Sirens and walks away. He has spotted Boylan again, and instead of flinching, decides to pursue him into the Ormond Hotel. This sudden resolve so distracts Bloom that he forgets to pay for the stationery for another letter to Martha—a gesture that reduces her to a lackluster Siren and re-instates Molly's importance. As his thoughts follow the departing Boylan to his own front door and the meeting with Molly, Bloom thinks, "All is lost." But for the first time he thinks of change: "Too late now. Or if not? . . . If still?" He bears no hate, Joyce says. Resolve and forgiveness define Bloom at this moment. He leaves, resisting the barmaid Sirens, and moments later pretends not to see a familiar prostitute on the street. Confronted with an image of diminished life, Bloom chooses to resist—a decision linking him to Stephen. Joyce calls Bloom an "unconquered hero." The chapter is presented ingeniously in language as music. Joyce guides are especially helpful here.

Chapter XII— "The Cyclops"

The cave-dwelling one-eyed giant Clyclops hurled in vain a rock at Odysseus' departing ship. The Cyclops in Chapter XII is a mean-spirited myopic bully whose Irish nationalism would evict all English and Jewish invaders. The chapter, written as it might have been spoken aloud in Barney Kiernan's pub with the ferocious citizen and his disagreeable dog at the center, prompts laughing-out-loud. Bloom's benign purpose for being in the pub is to join Paddy Dignam's friends in securing insurance for his widow. Inadvertently he enrages the citizen and responds to the ensuing explosion of hostility with his doctrine of universal brotherhood which is met by this crowd with scorn. Bloom later states, in an unusual moment of confident self-assertion, that both Jesus and Mendelssohn were Jews. This reasonable remark prompts the citizen to hurl a biscuit tin at Bloom and he is ushered out by Cunningham. Vision and blindness and much stylistic virtuosity fill this chapter. "A nation is the same people living in the same place," says Bloom—another reasonable observation with continuing relevance.

Chapter XIII— "Nausicaa"

After this disturbing assault, Bloom retreats to Sandymount Strand where, earlier, Stephen has walked. Here Bloom encounters Gerty MacDowell, a young woman on the beach caretaking small children. Gerty is an inexact Nausicaa, the princess who discovers and cares for Odysseus on the beach. Gerty's language exposes the farcical sentimentality of supermarket romance novels. Privately, she feigns emotion for effect (she practices crying "nicely" in front of the mirror) and her sentimentality turns Bloom into an aristocratic romantic stranger—a distortion as inaccurate as the zenophobic citizen's. The perversely pure and prurient Gerty deliberately exposes her leg to entice Bloom to masturbate. Leaving, she imagines they will meet again—a harsh observation by Joyce that some Dubliners have more of a life in the fantasies they imagine others have of them. Gerty's clichés contrast with Bloom's complexity: his watch has stopped inexplicably at 4:30, the hour he knows Molly is with Boylan and he calls Gerty a "devil" while feeling sympathy for her lameness. Masturbation provides Bloom some relief but he suggests its wasteful inefficacy by being uneasy about returning home. Bloom returns despondently to thoughts of Molly and decides to not blame Boylan. Before leaving the beach Bloom writes enigmatically in the sand: "I. AM. A."

Chapter XIV— "The Oxen of the Sun"

Bloom proceeds to the Lying-In Hospital to check on Mrs. Purefoy who has delivered a son. It is ten in the evening. Bloom hears the medical students, with Stephen and Lynch (from *Portrait*), irreverently discussing fertility themes. The sacred oxen of the sun are linked to fertility, and Odysseus' men are killed for disobeying the order not to eat them. Mulligan, divorcing love from sex, offers to perform like a stallion on a human breeding farm. As if to signify God's anger at debasing the holy view of conception, a great crash of thunder startles the group. Stephen becomes subdued as if recognizing in the thunder a power greater than human. Already drunk, he proposes to become more so and invites the others to Burke's pub. Bloom, sensing Stephen will soon need paternal protection, follows him but not before sending congratulations to Mrs. Purefoy—an especially generous gesture considering his sadness about Rudy. It is possible that Joyce saved the brewing crack of thunder for the moment that sets Stephen and Bloom on the same path. Many critics believe both are importantly changed by their interaction. The chapter, focusing on the evolution of the embryo, is written in language that follows the evolution of style. This literary device may also reflect Joyce's interest in multiple perspectives: world view is organized by the choice of language depicting it. The final voice of the chapter is the oratory of an American evangelist—another character with fearsomely rigid views.

Chapter XV— "Circe"

Odysseus escaped the curse of Circe, the enchantress, by carrying a charmed plant, but his men were turned into swine. Bloom follows Stephen to Dublin's Nighttown where, under the spell of alcohol and fatigue, they yield to their inner perversions, fantasies, and fears. The chapter (longest in the book) is presented as a series of hallucinations and the scenes are fantastic: Bloom's soap has personality; buttons speak; and The End of the World dances into the room. The reader has difficulty distinguishing actual from imagined events. Bloom sees young Rudy and Stephen sees his dead mother. Both sightings seem like genuine ghost experiences and they differ from the dream-like overlapping of images, memories, and objects. Stephen falls under Circe's spell—the brothel of Bella Cohen—but flees, guilt-stricken by the image of his still-loving mother, after breaking Bella's chandelier. Bloom pays Bella and rushes out to find Stephen in the menacing presence of two drunk British soldiers who, incapable of reasonable interaction, knock Stephen down. Bloom hovers over Stephen and calls him by name. The image of Rudy appears as the sweet eleven-year-old he might have become.

Bloom seems to enlarge his unceasing love for Rudy to include Stephen as a son of his soul. Rudy wears a reminder of the lambs-wool corselet woven by Molly. In the formless darkness of Night-town, it is a radiant moment.

Chapter XVI— "Eumaeus"

This chapter begins the third section of *Ulysses*. Bloom leads Stephen to the nearest site for sustenance and shelter—the cabman's all-night stand for wayfarers of the night. Fatigued by the hour (one a.m.), Bloom and Stephen fall into conversation that puts them comically at odds and reveals Bloom's incomplete education. They agree about nationalism and universal brotherhood and recognize a mutual affinity. The chapter is also about disguises and imposters. Odysseus arrives in Ithaca unrecognized by his loyal herdsman (Eumaeus) and reunites with Telemachus to plan the ousting of Penelope's suitors. The proprietor of the cabman's shelter is linked uncertainly with the Phoenix Park murder which falsely implicated Parnell. The mariner Munchausen sails under false colors. Even the mysterious "Macintosh," identified only by his coat and now named M'Intosh, is wrongly included in the list of mourners at Paddy Dignam's funeral, whereas Bloom appears as "L. Boom." The for-lorn hope that Parnell is still alive fits here as well. Bloom shows Stephen alluring pictures of Molly and invites him home for a cup of Epps's cocoa. But the connections between Stephen and Bloom are never sentimentalized. As in real life (unlike romance novels) barriers persist between people. These last three chapters corre-spond in style with the first three. Here, the narrator is suitable to the old men who dominate the scene in contrast to the young voices in the tower. The personal catechism in "Nestor" contrasts with the impersonal catechism of the upcoming "Ithaca." Stephen's male monologue on the beach in "Proteus" matches Molly's female monologue in "Penelope."

Chapter XVII— "Ithaca"

The reader is abruptly catapulted to the perspective of the stars. From vast and empty space, Stephen and Bloom, walking home along the dark streets in their imperfect union, look insignificant, and the impulse to ask "Is anyone out there benignly watching us?"

hovers over the chapter. The second paragraph lists topics discussed on the way which represent the range of activity that human beings put against the vastness: art, religion, relationship, and all the ongoing fascination with the observed world. The literary technique is the impersonal question and answer of scientific inquiry in which human emotion is not so much deflated as expunged. Keyless Bloom has to enter his home through a back door like the disguised Odysseus. He serves Stephen generously and invites him to spend the night. Stephen declines. Before departing into the near-dawn, he stands with Bloom as they urinate on the lawn and both are confronted with a spectacle that instantly fills the void with poetic beauty: "the heaventree of stars hung with humid nightblue fruit." The scientific method did not produce that image. Odysseus returns to Ithaca to kill the suitors. Nonviolent Bloom, contemplating his jealousy of Boylan, destroys his rival by shifting his perspective. Under the influence of stars, Bloom responds with equanimity instead of rage, deflating Boylan by choosing to regard his intrusion as transient and less calamitous than suns colliding with planets, less reprehensible than theft or cruelty to animals, and, finally, as merely "natural." He plans no retaliation; he defeats Boylan by making him irrelevant. Unordinary Bloom functions here like the kidney in the body, neutralizing and expelling the ambient toxins—an unglamorous organ in the Body of Christ. The chapter ends with a dot on the page signifying the place where all wanderers return. The famous dot can be variously interpreted as dust, the earth, nowhere-at-all, a womb, or matter materializing out of nowhere. It suggests at least the first miracle: there is something rather than nothing.

Chapter XVIII— "Penelope"

The final chapter shifts perspective again—this time to Molly, who has been present in the novel only in the minds of men, especially Bloom's. The reader moves from the distant stars to a warm bed on earth. The chapter consists of eight unpunctuated segments of Molly's interior thought as she lies, restlessly awake, head to toe with the sleeping Bloom. She begins by pondering the mundane mystery of Bloom's unprecedented request that she serve breakfast to him in bed the next morning. Details of the day, especially involving her various men—past, present, and future—dominate Molly's thoughts. She is an inexact Penelope, not technically faithful and certainly not patient, but Boylan in her view is a flawed lover and person in a way that she acknowledges Bloom is not, and she has no plans to leave her husband. The reader may be confused about which man she is thinking about, but in the end it is clearly Bloom that she returns to with her accepting "yes." The personality of Molly offends some traditional women and feminists alike—the former because of her frank and uninhibited enjoyment of sex and the latter because she is too preoccupied with men. She is certainly linked to the feminine principles of creation and connectedness but she is also unusual in having something of her own career. She engages us with her realistic assessments of men and unGerty-like acceptance of the less delicate aspects of being a woman. Molly's disdain for the worlds of politics and rational discourse may simultaneously offend and relieve the reader who has made the painstaking efforts to explain life and experienced some of the contentiousness and isolation as a consequence. Like Bloom she is disdainful of rancour and all forms of violence. In traditional novels there is generally a narrative purpose that compels action and produces change. In *Ulysses* there is action and some change but there is mainly the ordinary fullness of life itself to which Molly, and presumably Joyce, says "yes." ❀

Critical Views on
Ulysses

THORNTON WILDER ON PARTICULARITY AND
UNIVERSALITY IN *ULYSSES*

[Thornton Wilder (1897–1975) won the Pulitzer Prize for
Literature in 1938 for his play *Our Town*. He was the
Charles Eliot Norton Professor at Harvard in 1950–51. In
his lecture, "Joyce and the Modern Novel," included in *A
James Joyce Miscellany* (1957), Wilder asks the question:
Why did Joyce have to write in such a difficult way? He
speaks about Joyce's need for a style that would reveal each
individual as both sole and unique and also archetypal.]

In addition, there is an obsessive compulsion toward the all-inclusive
—what you might call the kitchen stove complex. He will get everything in there including the kitchen stove if he possibly can. It is a
sort of need to make the catalogue absolutely complete. Not a dozen,
but every one of the sutras of the Koran ⟨. . .⟩ every one of the Saints
in the calendar. ⟨. . .⟩

How, as a literary method, does he render an individual archetypi-
cally? Joyce was fundamentally a great realistic writer. ⟨. . .⟩

Now, you and I and everybody live a complete life under unique
occasions. Every single moment of our life is unique in that sense.
Every human being lives only unique occasions, just as we all die one
death—our death and no one else's. Likewise, of the millions of
times that "I love" has been said, each time it is really said just once.
The participation in essential love or essential death is, as they now
are saying "Existential,"—totally individual.

The realistic novel is the art of these unique occasions. ⟨. . .⟩

The realistic method ⟨. . .⟩ was Joyce's point of departure. He
wanted not to tell how Mr. So-and-so met Miss So-and-so and
how they got married in such and such a place. It was this kind of
realization that led to a search for a new way of making it arresting
to us. ⟨. . .⟩

You have lost some husband, brother, or parent in the war. Your grief is very real to you. Yet now we know as never before that a great many died in this war and in the wars of Carthage and Troy and Ur, and in the Thirty Years War—what end is there to any human thing in which you are not also companion to billions? It does not diminish your grief but it orients it to a larger field of reference.

This shift in outlook brings two results. We are less interested in the anecdote, in the "plot," Mr. So-and-so met the attractive Miss So-and-so. We wish them well; but the mere account of their progress no longer arrests us in the same way. ⟨. . .⟩

Plot must be stated differently in order to arrest the attention. ⟨. . .⟩

The second result is an urgent search for the validity of individual experience. Though I realize that my joy or my grief is but "one" in the ocean of human life, nevertheless it *has* its reality. I know that the existential thing pouring up in me, my joy or my fear, is a real thing and yet that the intensity with which I feel it can be called absurd. It is absurd to claim that "I," in the vast reaches of time and place and repetition, is worth an assertion. ⟨. . .⟩

Now Joyce is that great novelist of these two things. He is the novelist who has most succeeded in placing man in an immense field of reference, among all the people who have lived and died, in all the periods of time, all the geography of the world, all the races, all the catastrophes of history. And he is also the one who has most dramatically engaged in a search for the validity of the individual as an absolute. ⟨. . .⟩

All these devices were necessary to "orient" the individual within the universe. To them one ingredient more has been added: Joyce was a great comic genius. The comic spirit is constantly relieving us of the burden of life's logical implications. Confront life logically and you might as well resign at once. Human beings cannot bear much wrong and cannot bear much logic and they cannot bear too much self-examination; and the comic spirit was given to us as reconciliation and as an alibi from drawing the last deductions. ⟨. . .⟩

—Thornton Wilder, "Joyce and the Modern Novel." In *A James Joyce Miscellany,* ed., Marvin Magalaner (New York: James Joyce Society, 1957): pp. 12–15, 17–18.

S. L. Goldberg on Irony

[S. L. Goldberg's book, *The Classical Temper* (1961), is one of the classics in Joyce scholarship. After summarizing the views of some earlier critics who saw depicted in *Ulysses* a materialistic and demoralized society, Goldberg argues that Joyce's view of the world is too complex and complete to support that assessment.]

The most obvious mode of irony in *Ulysses* is the exposure of the protagonists' inadequacies and contradictions, the sharp, diagnostic irony that underlies Joyce's comparison of the noble and spacious world of Homer with the flaccid corruption of the present. Bloom and Stephen represent a disfigurement of the spirit for all to see, each, in his isolation, typical of a world in which everyone seems lost. Bloom's hopes and ambitions (like Stephen's pretentious egotism) are symbols of a universal decay. He is the suffering and excluded victim of a society he embodies in himself, and in "Circe" the two sides of his being arise and do battle within him. Stephen is also the victim of what he rejects. Guilt-ridden, sterile, conceited, kinetic, he embodies the very failures he so bitterly criticizes in the world around him. He seems to reject only because he is rejected. Together, the two men comprise the disintegration of "an age of whoredom groping for its god", their "heroism" a pathetic mockery of the firm, marvellous freshness of the Homeric dawn.

But there is another kind of irony, another side to the Homeric analogy. There are equally genuine parallels between the resourceful, insinuating, multi-faceted heroes of the *Odyssey* and *Ulysses*, between the common life of men and women in one age and the other, even between the gusto and vivacity of the two books; and these complicate and modify the mock-heroic perspective. The various effects of the Homeric parallels, as Mr. Kenner's own excellent analysis of them shows, cannot be summed up in any one neat formula, for Joyce's irony is by no means directed simply at the shortcomings of the present age. By disregarding the conventional plaster draperies on the figure of Ulysses, by insisting on the absurd, vulgar confusion of life, Joyce's irony also cuts back on the supposed grandiosities of the past in order to reveal the living clay of humanity in every age. Hence the ambiguities of *Ulysses*, which seems at once a satirical caricature of the world and a clear-eyed, realistic portrait, a cry for the New Jerusalem and a tear for dear dirty Dublin. But Dublin is any city, Bloomsday any day—by concentrating on the ordinary Joyce makes his generalizations—and neither if they were supremely good nor unless they were good could they be corrupted. The citizens of his city are not saints, and not many even aspire to be. They are as good as they may be. They live and partly live; they perceive truth imperfectly; they realize their values in part; in all, they do no better nor worse than the citizens of any world, Homer's or Dante's. They are not all saved, nor are they irretrievably damned.

—S. L. Goldberg, *The Classical Temper* (London: Chatto and Windus, 1961): pp. 118–119.

S. L. GOLDBERG ON STEPHEN'S VIEW OF HISTORY

[In this extract from "Homer and the Nightmare of History" in *The Argument of Ulysses* Goldberg focuses on the "Nestor" chapter where Stephen reveals the existential questions about history that preoccupy him.]

⟨. . .⟩ And the main theme of the chapter is Stephen's hostility to, and fear of, the past. Time seems to him only to repeat itself in "the same room and hour, the same wisdom. . . . Three nooses round me here", or in the repeated experience of the Jews:

> Time surely would scatter all. A hoard heaped by the roadside: plundered and passing on. Their eyes knew the years of wandering and, patient, knew the dishonours of their flesh.
> —Who has not? Stephen said.

In short, "history was a tale like any other too often heard". The individual seems helplessly bound to the pattern; the "dear might of Him that walked the waves" does not exist for Stephen. He can see as little in the present as he can see in Elizabethan England—"an age of exhausted whoredom groping for its god". The ages, as John Eglinton puts it, seem only to "succeed one another" without change or hope. So conceived, history must seem a nightmare.

—History, Stephen said, is a nightmare from which I am trying to awake.

From the playfield the boys raised a shout. A whirring whistle: goal. What if that nightmare gave you a back kick?

—The ways of the Creator are not our ways, Mr Deasy said. All history moves towards one great goal, the manifestation of God.

Stephen jerked his thumb towards the window, saying:

—That is God.

Hooray! Ay! Whrrwhee!

—What? Mr Deasy asked.

—A shout in the street, Stephen answered, shrugging his shoulders.

Stephen cannot accept that history moves to any supernatural end outside itself. If God exists, He manifests Himself here and now, in all life however pointless or trivial it may seem. History is not like a detective story; there are no comforting revelations to follow. When Stephen uses teleological arguments himself later on, he does so only analogously for another and very different conclusion.

His obsessive fear of the past is partly balanced, however, by a different strain of thought about history. If past events limit the present and the future, they also, as acts of will, liberate possibilities into the world of fact. Stephen ponders this dual aspect of history in Aristotelian terms:

> Had Pyrrhus not fallen by a beldam's hand in Argos or Julius Caesar not been knifed to death. They are not to be thought away. Time has branded them and fettered they are lodged in the room of the infinite possibilities they have ousted. But can those have been possible seeing that they never were? Or was that only possible which came to pass? Weave, weaver of the wind.

And during the schoolboys' reading of *Lycidas,* the grounds of hope occur to him: time is not only a burden, it is also a means to the fruition and fulfilment of the soul in action. As he tells himself a little later, he could, if he willed it, break free of his present nooses—and in fact he does. History involves more than the ossification of life; it is also dynamic.

—S. L. Goldberg, *The Argument of Ulysses* (Columbus: Ohio State University Press, 1961): pp. 156–157.

STANLEY SULTAN ON THE RANGE OF VIEWS ABOUT THE
NOVEL UP TO 1964

[Stanley Sultan (b. 1928) teaches English at Clark University. He is the author of *The Argument of Ulysses* (1964), an extensive guide through the chapters. Sultan's thoughtful summary of the scholarship on *Ulysses* up to the time of his writing provides a good foundation for new Joyce scholars.]

⟨. . .⟩ The book clearly has a protagonist, yet there has been no generally accepted account of what he experiences or of what he does. No one has demonstrated conclusively how Mr. Bloom's Odyssey has ended, or even if it has ended. The development of his relations with the two other major characters is unclear; and thus, the fate the narrative indicates for all three principals is unclear. If there is a scandal connected with *Ulysses*, it relates to this striking fact.

The critical interpretations of the book reflect the situation: they are numerous and extend over the whole range of possibilities. One, and it is argued well only by Edmund Wilson, is that *Ulysses* ends happily, and therefore expresses an affirmative philosophy of life; another is that the author holds out hope for his protagonists although their condition is miserable, and therefore shows the human condition to be potentially positive; a third is that he presents with deep sympathy a pathetic world. In addition to affirmation, optimism, and commiseration, the book is thought to assert pessimism—a simple despair about life—and even nihilism—the author's attempt to discredit or destroy all traditional values of life and art.

These are the interpretations of critics who regard the book as fundamentally serious. Those who think it quite the opposite differ from one another in a corresponding way, with the determining consideration whether Joyce is seen to be: (a) involved with the characters and world of his comedy; or (b) outside that world ("the indifferent artist" "paring his fingernails") and mocking it. The more substantial interpretation in the first category is that the book is essentially positive because its heroic and mythic allusions ennoble rather than denigrate its commonplace modern world. The other considers it to be simply "genial and comic," the work of a "humorous writer of the traditional English school—in temper, at his best, very like Sterne." One interpretation in the second category represents the book as comic pessimism—pessimistic and not nihilistic because it asserts spiritual and moral values which its characters fail to live up to, comic because "To be able to laugh with others at the recognized absurdity of a common tangential position ["all men's sundering"] may be a first step in the direction of a reconciliation." Mostly, however, critics of this persuasion are among the many who find it nihilistic, even when they do not draw the conclusion themselves. Its essence "is God laughing at the world from which (as the Cabala tells us) he has withdrawn," its comic principle, "the hard cerebral ridicule of the ironist who has smashed through all the paper-walls of his environment and, turning suddenly, observed the essential filth of life. . . ."

Thus, the lack of general agreement about what happens in *Ulysses* is naturally reflected in a lack of general agreement about the nature and ultimate meaning of the book: it is called both comic and serious, both affirmative and negatory.

> —Stanley Sultan, *The Argument of Ulysses* (Columbus: Ohio State University Press, 1964): pp. 6–7.

ROBERT MARTIN ADAMS ON PUZZLING MOMENTS

[Robert Martin Adams (1924–1996) was a prodigious and distinguished scholar at Cornell. In his book *Surface and Symbol* (1967) Adams notes the profusion of details in *Ulysses* and highlights the frequency of puzzling moments—some of which resurface from time to time in the novel with no additional clarification. One amusing example is discussed in this extract.]

Perhaps the most disconcerting yet characteristic elements in Joyce's disconcerting novel are those patterns of thought and feeling which, like the Cheshire Cat or the Snark, are forever on the verge of disappearing. They may be there or they may not; if there, they may be significant or they may not; one is obtuse if one fails to recognize them, but silly and oversubtle if one makes too much of them. There is not enough assurance that meaning of any sort is intended, or for that matter that equivocation is being performed, for the reader to feel anything but uneasy.

For instance, in several sections of the book, Denis Breen is seen wandering about Dublin, deeply disturbed over a postcard someone has sent him. It contains simply the message "U.P. up," but he is prepared to sue the author, if he can discover him, for criminal libel. Under these circumstances, it presumably makes some difference what the message means, and many guesses have been put forward as to the imputation which has reduced Denis Breen to such a dither. Of course, there is always the possibility that it means nothing whatever; then Denis Breen is projecting his own mental disturbances upon an essential blank. But if the phrase "U.P. up" is a covert way of saying "you urinate," implying "you're no good," or if it implies that he puts his finger U.P. up his anus, he has somewhat more grounds for indignation. If it is a jeer at his sexual incapacity, "you can't get it U.P. up any more," he has still further reason for indignation, and we evidently have grounds for seeing the family life of the Breens as a sort of parallel with that of the Blooms. If it implies that the jig is "U.P. up," the card may be taken as a threat of blackmail; if it means, on the other hand, that it's all "U.P. up" with Mr. Breen, the card announces his approaching death, ties in with his dream of the ace of spades which is a symbol of death, and renders him pathetic. In effect, we cannot tell what, if anything, the card is a symbol of, until we know what it is as a surface; and about this Joyce has given us no adequate grounds for deciding. I have given five interpretations of it, and J. J. O'Molloy adds another when he says, "it implies that he is not *compos mentis*." We may find some grounds outside the novel for preferring one of these six meanings to the other five; for instance, on p. 2 of the *Freeman's Journal* for Thursday, November 5, 1903, appeared a report of a suit in which one McKettrick sued a man named Kiernan, for having sent him a libelous postcard. Maybe this has something to do with Denis Breen's behavior, though Kiernan's postcard did not say "U.P. up." On the other hand, the exact expression is used in Arnold Bennett's novel, the *Old Wives' Tale,* under circumstances which give it the last meaning indicated above; a doctor emerges from a sickroom, and announces "U.P. up," meaning evidently that it's all up with the patient.

—Robert Martin Adams, *Surface and Symbol* (USA: Galaxy Books, 1967): pp. 191–193.

FRITZ SENN ON GERTY MACDOWELL AND THE GIRL ON THE STRAND

[Fritz Senn is director of the research center at the Zurich International James Joyce Foundation and author of *Inductive Scrutinies: Focus on Joyce.* In his contribution to *James Joyce's* Ulysses: *Critical Essays* (1974) Senn looks at the "Nausicaa" chapter and points to the parallels in language and meaning between Bloom's episode with Gerty MacDowell and Stephen's with the girl on the strand in *Portrait.*]

Gerty MacDowell is the latest avatar of the temptress in Joyce's fiction. ⟨. . .⟩

A Portrait presents its own gallery of temptresses, leading up to the vision in Chapter 4 and the villanelle of Chapter 5. The girl who meets Stephen's gaze on the strand connects two otherwise separate strands of sensual eroticism and mariolatric images of purity. The similarity between this twilight scene and the portrait of Gerty MacDowell in *Ulysses* has often been remarked upon. ⟨. . .⟩

To realize just how much the 'Nausicaa' chapter metamorphoses elements of Stephen's ecstasy on the beach in *A Portrait,* it is worth collating a few images and phrases. Almost every item, for example, of the catalogue that describes the impression made on Stephen by the bird-girl has been re-used. Both girls are alone, gazing into the distant sea, aware of being watched, and in both cases there is mention of waist, bosom, hair, face, softness, drawers, skirts, slenderness, touch, shame, etc. Some specific transpositions are amusing. The 'magic' changing the girl into the likeness of a seabird is at work in 'Nausicaa' too, in the 'magic lure' in Gerty's eyes. The seabird may have become a 'canary bird', but Bloom himself thinks of 'seabirds.' The girl's legs are 'delicate'; delicacy is one of Gerty's strong points, extending to her hands, her flush (—flushes are part of the scenery in the *Portrait* too), and the 'pink' creeping into her pretty cheek. Since 'from everything in the least indelicate her finebred nature instinctively recoiled', she would be peeved to know that Bloom callously awards the palm of delicacy to her rival: 'That squinty one is delicate'. The ivory of the bird-girl's thighs is part of Gerty's make-up: 'ivorylike purity'. The term 'slateblue' contains Gerty's favourite colour, but Bloom uses 'on the slate' in quite another context. The 'ringdove' associated with Gerty's defiant voice may be compared to the 'dovelike' bosom of Stephen's vision, or to her skirts, which are 'dovetailed'. The 'worship' of Stephen's eyes has its counterpart in Bloom's 'dark eyes . . . literally worshipping at her shrine'. The 'faint flame' that trembled on the cheek of the girl in *A Portrait* is re-lit as a 'warm flush . . . surging and flaming into her [Gerty's] cheeks'. Even the precious word 'fashioned', which is used for the trail of seaweed in the earlier scene, seems to have been transferred from the literary tradition to the marketplace—to the ambit of 'Dame Fashion', one of Gerty's patron saints, whose call she follows as a 'votary', just as Stephen devoted himself to Art.

⟨. . .⟩ Gerty's climax could be called, as Stephen's in fact is, 'an outburst of profane joy'. Etymologically, 'profane' means 'outside the temple' (Lat. *fanum* = fane), which is exactly where the action on Sandymount strand takes place, literally near 'that simple fane beside the waves'.

⟨. . .⟩ The two episodes reflect on each other. In a sense, 'Nausicaa' continues the familiar technique of *A Portrait*, the repetition of an earlier event in a rearrangement, with a change of tone and a new slant (often amounting to a disillusionment) brought about, very often, by a reshuffling of the same verbal material with some additional twists of phraseology. The reading experience is characterized by shifts of perspective (one of the structural devices of *Ulysses*), which should also make us wary of singling out any one of the stages in the process of cognition, however convincing, as the decisive one.

—Fritz Senn, *James Joyce's* Ulysses: *Critical Essays,* eds., Clive Hart and David Hayman (Berkeley and Los Angeles California: University of California Press, 1974): pp. 284–286.

[Richard Ellmann (1918–1987) wrote extensively on Joyce
(including his famous biography *James Joyce*, 1959) as well
on William Butler Yeats (*The Identity of Yeats*, 1964). In this
extract from *The Consciousness of Joyce* (1977), Ellmann
looks at the old issue of the place (if any) for political perspective in art.]

Apologists for his Catholicism have pointed out that he repudiates
the Church in *A Portrait* only to the degree that it impinges upon his
hero, and not absolutely. But that is merely to say that he keeps
within the frame of his fiction; it does not reduce the authority of
Stephen as a model. Joyce's attitude towards the State has also been
misinterpreted, not least by Marxist critics. At the Congress of
Writers in Kharkov in 1933, Karl Radek accused him of being a
defender of bourgeois capitalism, and some non-Marxist critics,
reading *Ulysses* the same way, have marvelled at what they take to be
Joyce's complacency about the social order, or what Lionel Trilling
has called his indifference to politics. ⟨. . .⟩ S. L. Goldberg has
lamented that Joyce failed in *Ulysses* to display the evils of modern
industrialism as D. H. Lawrence in *Women in Love* exposed the horrors of the coal mines. ⟨. . .⟩ Yet Joyce was not altogether at a loss
because of the lack of heavy industry in his country. He used instead
as his principal emblem of modern capitalism the newspaper,
wasting the spirit with its peristent attacks upon the integrity of the
word, narcotizing its readers with superficial facts, habituating them
to secular and clerical authority. ⟨. . .⟩

His own function was that of a sentry sounding an alarm, in the
name of what in *Stephen Hero* he called "a new humanity, active,
unafraid and unashamed." As he said there,

> He wished to express his nature freely and fully for the
> benefit of a society which he would enrich and also for his
> own benefit, seeing that it was part of his life to do so. It
> was not part of his life to attempt an extensive alteration of
> society but he felt the need to express himself such an
> urgent need, such a real need, that he was determined no
> conventions of a society, however plausibly mingling pity
> with its tyranny should be allowed to stand in his way, and

though a taste for elegance and detail unfitted him for the part of a demagogue, from his general attitude he might have been supposed not unjustly an ally of the collectivist politicians, who are often very seriously upbraided by opponents who believe in Jehovahs, and decalogues and judgments with sacrificing the reality to an abstraction.

⟨. . .⟩ To catch the conscience of the people in his book must be his motive. Literature is a revolutionary instrument, however roundabout it may move. ⟨. . .⟩

Ulysses provides a measure against which British State and Catholic Church can be evaluated, and Ireland as well, both in its patent collusion with these forces, and in the callousness which the desire for independence could evoke. If British tyranny was brutally materialistic, so was Irish fanaticism. Persecution, by Church or by State, whether of Jews or of artists, went with other forms of materialism, such as sexual cruelty and lovelessness. On the other side was an etherealism which included the diseased ideals of religion and patriotism, ideals without body and essences without form, antisexualism or love cheapened by sentimentality. ⟨. . .⟩

⟨. . .⟩ While neither Bloom nor Stephen offers a coherent programme of change, neither is satisfied with simply laying bare the inadequacies of Irish spiritual and secular governors. Stephen is bent upon affirming, and needling his compatriots into affirming, the disused possibilities of life. He wants them to walk untrammelled by petrified dogmas. For Bloom what is truly life is love, possibly a crude term for his sense of mutuality of concern but at least a traditional one. As a young man he was a socialist, and annoyed Molly during their early acquaintance by informing her that Christ was the first socialist. The Church he finds bloodthristy and prone to make victims, the State the same. ⟨. . .⟩

—Richard Ellmann, *The Consciousness of Joyce* (Toronto and New York: Oxford University Press, 1970): pp. 77–82.

COLIN MACCABE ON A WITTY TREATMENT OF A SERIOUS THEME

[Colin MacCabe taught at Cambridge University and Strath-clyde University in Glasgow. He is a professor of nineteenth- and twentieth-century literature at the University of Pittsburgh and chair of the English department at the University of Exeter. MacCabe wrote *The Eloquence of the Vulgar: Language, Cinema, and the Politics of Culture* (1999) and co-edited with Cornell West *White Screens, Black Images: Holly-wood from the Dark Side* (1994). He is also the editor of *James Joyce, New Perspectives* (1982). In his book *James Joyce and the Revolution of the Word* (1979), MacCabe focuses on Stephen's difficulty establishing a stable identity for his own "I" and then gives an amusing example from "Scylla and Charybdis" of a metaphysical way to resolve an identity problem when it takes the form of a debt Stephen owes to A. E. (the poet George Russell). Instability briefly has its benefits.]

> How now, sirrah, that pound he lent you when you were hungry?
> Marry, I wanted it.
> Take thou this noble.
> Go to! You spent most of it in Georgina Johnson's bed, clergyman's daughter. Agenbite of inwit.
> Do you intend to pay it back?
> O, yes.
> When? Now?
> Well . . . no.
> When, then?
> I paid my way. I paid my way.
> Steady on. He's from beyant Boyne water. The northeast corner. You owe it.
> Wait. Five months. Molecules all change. I am other I now. Other I got pound.
> Buzz. Buzz.
> But I, entelechy, form of forms, am I by memory because under everchanging forms.
> I that sinned and prayed and fasted.
> A child Conmee saved from pandies.
> I, I, and I. I.
> A.E.I.O.U.

Stephen's longing to establish an immutable 'I' for himself is paralleled by his attempt to allocate Shakespeare a definite position in the plays. Stephen wishes to centre Shakespeare's life in the moment when Anne Hathaway tumbled him in the cornfield and then to centre the plays in turn through the interpretation of *Hamlet*. For Stephen, *Hamlet* must be read from the position of the ghost, from the character which he imagines that Shakespeare acted and from whose situation he constructs the meaning of Shakespeare's life and plays. In this search for meaning, Stephen must ignore chance as depriving a life of the coherence necessary for any interpretation. When John Eglington has the temerity to introduce chance into the discussion, 'The world believes that Shakespeare made a mistake and got out of it as quickly and as best he could', Stephen angrily splutters, 'Bosh! A man of genius makes no mistakes. His errors are volitional and are the portals of discovery.' Stephen wishes to tie every event within a life to the will and thus avoid the admission of chance. The next line of the text, however, emphasises the arbitrary when it mockingly declares 'Portals of discovery opened to let in the quaker librarian, soft-creakfooted, bald, eared and assiduous'. As Stephen sits in the corner of the library at the imaginary centre of his world, that world is constantly being altered by events outside his control. It is chance that will confront him with Bloom later in the day as it is chance that brings Bloom through the library doors a few minutes later.

The neurotic's denial of chance is at one with the denial of the signifier. Both threaten identity, leaving it at the mercy of others' actions and others' voices. ⟨. . .⟩ He complains that 'I am tired of my voice, the voice of Esau. My kingdom for a drink'. The voice of Esau, as the Bible tells us, is the voice that cannot establish identity, that is not sufficient to ensure paternal recognition. Stephen's difficulty is that he cannot find a figure that can occupy the place of the father. If the real father's weakness prevents an identification, the imaginary father of the nation is an equally impotent being who lacks both a living language and political independence. Neither can function as an origin secure enough to guarantee his present identity, abandoning him to the mercy of chance and language.

It is this reality of chance and language that Stephen's theory of Shakespeare, a theory of origin and identity, repudiates. Stephen's rejection of his own theory signals a liberation from the neurotic problematic within which he had constructed Shakespeare's biography. Caught in the contradiction that his theory must hold for all of Shakespeare's plays, but that he has not read all the plays, Stephen laughs 'to free his mind from his mind's bondage'. It is with this laugh that he disowns the attempt to characterise Shakespeare's work as a representation of Shakespeare's life. ⟨. . .⟩

⟨. . .⟩ Stephen's laugh, however, is not produced by a simple mistake but in the realisation that any statement is always mistaken in so far as there is always more information available. ⟨. . .⟩

—Colin MacCabe, *Joyce and the Revolution of the Word* (London and Basingstoke: The MacMillan Press, 1979): pp. 118–121.

COLIN MACCABE ON LANGUAGE AS A TOOL FOR DIVISIVENESS IN "CYCLOPS"

[In this extract from *James Joyce and the Revolution of the Word* MacCabe discusses the "practice of listing" which is one way division is created between people.]

⟨. . .⟩ To list is to apply a set of identities to the world and it is the power of language to produce lists, to articulate a set of divisions, which is the power to produce a world for the senses. The lists within the text are all, in some sense, ruined; deprived of their ability to disappear and reveal the world. Instead, it is writing which dominates the scene. The continuous setting up of differences, the endless production of identities and sense—it is this which constitutes the text of the Cyclops. ⟨. . .⟩

⟨. . .⟩ For Bloom, unlike the Citizen and the Nameless One, is not fixed within one discourse but participates pleasurably in several. Thus, in the brief time he is in the pub, he enters into the discourses of science and law as well as those of Irish nationalism and human compassion. Bloom's entry into the play of languages means that he cannot erect a fixed representation of the world which will explain the other languages. When asked to define what life really is he comes out with: 'Love, says Bloom. I mean the opposite of hatred. I must go now . . .'. Bloom refuses to stay to define the identity of life, to represent and to fix it. What is opposed to the violence of the citizen (based as it is on a fixed representation of the world) and the verbal violence of the Nameless One (also founded in a fixity of meaning) is the joyful entering into the various ways of signifying world and self. This is both Bloom's activity in the text and the activity of the reader in reading the text.

The insistence on a dominant discourse can be linked specifically to violence. The Citizen's violence in the text arises from the misunderstanding of Bloom's remark to Bantam Lyons that he was just going to throw his newspaper away. This remark can only be given one interpretation, one identity, by the betting fraternity of Dublin. It can only be represented in one way and it is this fixed interpretation that leads to violence. The Cyclops section is that part of *Ulysses* which is concerned with the eye and with sight. What we recognise as we read through the juxtaposition of various discourses is that the world we see is determined by the discourses we speak. Our senses and our sense are one. ⟨. . .⟩ But there is no discourse which sees everything, no discourse which will epiphanise the world in some total moment. Furthermore it is action based on this illusion of a final fixed reality which is allied in the Cyclops (as elsewhere in *Ulysses*) with violence and intolerance.

—Colin MacCabe, *James Joyce and the Revolution of the Word* (London and Basingstoke: The MacMillan Press, 1979): pp. 99, 101–2.

John Paul Riquelm on Shifting Perspectives in "Calypso"

[Ambiguity in *Ulysses* is commonly encountered by readers at all levels. In this extract from *Teller and Tale in Joyce's Fiction*, John Paul Riquelme discusses Joyce's skill in combining narrated and quoted monologue that shifts between the character's voice and a third person teller of the tale. Such shifts produce incongruities that surprise and entertain the reader.]

Often the teller shifts from a third-person perspective to the first person by employing language we can take in two ways, as in the following passage presenting Bloom's leaving the house for the butcher's: "On the doorstep he felt in his hip pocket for the latchkey. Not there. In the trousers I left off. Must get it." There is no clear distinction here between scene and psyche, though the shift from grammatically complete to grammatically incomplete statements may encourage us to make such a distinction. Even in the first sentence, we are in the character's mind, since only Bloom can know what he feels for, though "pocket" and "latchkey" have physical referents. The effect is like that of the adjective "untonsored" at the beginning of "Telemachus." We find out what one of the characters fails to discover in the scene. The teller also evokes Bloom's mind by a linguistic slippage, through the use of a verb that could introduce a presentation of thought in psycho-narration but that does not in context. Here "felt" negotiates an elision between a physical act, sense perception, and thought. The teller observes a physical act, Bloom's *feeling* for something that, when his sense of touch does not find it, Bloom *feels* he "must get." Teller and character share the burden of narration through the shift from feeling to feelings that evokes sense perception triggering thought. And we share that burden as well insofar as we expect "felt" to introduce thought.

Such a shift from description to thought becomes comic when the elision is less gradually modulated than in the passage about the key. For instance, as Bloom leaves we learn that he takes his hat down from its peg:

> His hand took his hat from the peg over his initialled heavy overcoat, and his lost property office secondhand waterproof. Stamps: stickyback pictures. Daresay lots of officers are in the swim too. Course they do. The sweated legend in the crown of his hat told him mutely: Plasto's high grade ha. He peeped quickly inside the leather headband. White slip of paper. Quite safe.

The first sentence seems straightforward enough, but its two parts are virtually antithetical in focus. The first one deals with the discrete details of physical scene: Bloom's hand, his hat, the peg, the coat that is initialled and heavy. The only detail that we cannot account for visually is the word "initialled," suggesting perhaps that Bloom's initials are inside the coat somewhere. Only Bloom could know that, not any teller simply reporting scene. We probably would pass over "initialled," except that the remainder works the same way, revealing what only Bloom could know while creating the effect of a physical description. We hear as if it were descriptive what no observer except Bloom could realize about his waterproof: not that it is brown, dirty, torn, or wrinkled, but that he obtained it secondhand at a lost property office. The second sentence using the third person and past tense, the one that reports what Bloom sees inside the hat, also engages the reader's attention in a special way, because it fails to do what the earlier sentence does: supplement the perception of scene with thought. Bloom knows already what the reader is asked to figure out: that the "t" of the word "hat" has been worn away. We learn what Bloom knows when we add what the hat mutely tells Bloom to what the narrator tells us; Bloom is looking into a hat, not into a "ha." Our response includes another sort of "ha" as well as an "aha."

—John Paul Riquelme, *Teller and Tale in Joyce's Fiction* (Baltimore and London: Johns Hopkins University Press, 1983): pp. 179–180.

DAVID A. WHITE ON METAPHYSICAL QUESTIONS
IN "HADES"

[David A. White produced his study of Joyce, *The Grand Continuum: Reflections on Joyce and Metaphysics* (1983), after teaching a course on Joyce and the philosophy of language at the New School for Social Research in 1978. In this extract White asks questions about the nature of language and consciousness. He uses four illustrations from *Ulysses*. One is discussed here.]

⟨. . .⟩ I have chosen to construe *Ulysses* as implicitly posing a series of fundamental questions concerning the relation between language and human consciousness, ultimately between language and being, insofar as consciousness exemplifies one part of being. From the standpoint of metaphysics, we shall concentrate on the problem of the primacy of flux, in particular by trying to identify different types of consciousness as they become present within linguistic transcriptions. ⟨. . .⟩

As examples of Joyce's style in *Ulysses*, I will cite four excerpts from the novel, then paraphrase and comment on the scope and types of consciousness treated in each one. Once we examine these excerpts in close conjunction with one another, their diversity should impress on us even more forcefully the need to scrutinize the "stream of consciousness" method to discern, for example, identity and difference within the boundaries of the possible isomorphism between language and consciousness. ⟨. . .⟩

⟨. . .⟩ Many thoughts pass through Bloom's mind as the body of his friend Patrick Dignam is about to be lowered into the ground:

> Shades of night hovering here with all the dead stretched about. The shadows of the tombs when churchyards yawn and Daniel O'Connell must be a descendant I suppose who is this used to say he was queer breedy man great catholic all the same like a big giant in the dark. Will o' the wisp. Gas of graves. Want to keep her mind off it to conceive at all. Woman especially are so touchy.

The passage begins on a very literary note; Bloom's somewhat lyrical observation could be an impersonal narrative account of what one might experience in a cemetery at night. However, the next sentence is intricately suggestive of consciousness at its most streaming. Bloom sees the shadows of the tombs and is instantly reminded of a salient image from *Hamlet,* his consciousness quickly moving from raw perception to involuted memory and imagination. But then he notices the tomb of a specific individual, apparently related to someone whom Bloom and the funeral entourage had just been discussing, and he conjectures on the possible blood relation between the two. Such speculation fades away as he sees something else, probably another tomb, one bearing the bones of an unknown deceased. But the known takes precedence over the unknown, and Bloom returns to report what had been voiced concerning the living relation of the deceased. Visual perception then becomes imaginative again in separate (and alliterative) evocations of a shadowy graveyard viewed at night. The sight of dead men flashes to the memory of living women, in particular their natural capacity for conceiving new life and, according to Bloom's ruminations, their equally natural reaction to the process in general. Once more, the present purely visual field has faded before associations held in Bloom's memory and evaluative judgments based on these memories. ⟨. . .⟩

—David A. White, *The Grand Continuum: Reflections on Joyce and Metaphysics* (Pittsburgh: University of Pittsburgh Press, 1983): pp. 108, 110–111.

ZACK BOWEN ON THE CHARACTER OF LEOPOLD BLOOM

[Zack Bowen is professor of English and chair of the English Department at the University of Delaware. He published *Musical Allusions in the Works of James Joyce* (1974) and he is the producer-director of Works by James Joyce for Folkway Records. In his essay on *Ulysses* that appears in *Companion to Joyce Studies* (1984), Bowen joins the critics who praise the essential and ordinary goodness in Bloom's complex personality.]

In Joyce's Odyssean parallel, Bloom has a wife who is indeed unfaithful. Unlike Odysseus, Bloom has not been successful at anything. He has failed to make a deal on a single advertisement during the day; his rhetoric has persuaded no one, and he is held in wide contempt rather than respect; and he is a bad dissembler and certainly not much at fighting. How, then, is this prime example of the anti-hero to be compared to Odysseus, beyond the fact that their marital situations and their wandering are roughly comparable? For one thing, Bloom is a pleasant person with a basically optimistic attitude. His schemes for social good and his continued relationship with his wife, his hopes for finding a son, his contempt for Boylan, his ability to survive and content himself with fantasies, masturbation, and hope, his practicality, his wisdom, his sense of humor, his knowledge of his own identity, his compassion, and, above all, his great sense of equanimity raise him to epic proportions. Bloom is not an ordinary man, nor are the events of his day ordinary, though, paradoxically, his life seems to follow a common pattern.

Few characters in literature have been developed so completely as has Leopold Bloom. The reader gets to know him through his stream-of-conscious thought, his subconscious fears, hopes, and aspirations, and his image in the opinion of others, culminating in his wife's drowsy ruminations. The character who emerges is a sort of amalgam of hapless pariah and comic messianic figure related to Christ, Parnell, and Moses—a would-be political savior of Ireland. The Irish have long had a tradition of looking for someone to lead them out of their bondage. This theme links Bloom and Stephen Dedalus, who has, throughout *A Portrait of the Artist* and certainly in *Ulysses*, shared the messianic aspiration.

Bloom is also a dreamer. He conjures up both the halcyon days of the past and visions of a future Eden with Molly in a kind of Eastern Utopia. Yet he is an eminently practical man, in touch with nature and himself, enjoying defecation, flatulence, and his general bodily functions. Bloom is a scientist, albeit off the track and uncomprehending most of the time, but possessed of scientific curiosity and endowed with a rudimentary knowledge of physics in particular. Bloom is also a social economist, willing to propose and implement schemes such as communal kitchens for the poor, compounded mandatory savings for each newborn, and a number of other schemes for the social good. He is a cross between a realistic messiah and a parody of ineffectuality. His theories are not quite absurd enough to dismiss completely and usually not quite practical enough ever to have a chance at implementation. This ambiguous borderline between comic and realistic renders Bloom a modern version of Don Quixote, except that, unlike the Don, Bloom is never deluded; as both modern hero and anti-hero, he begins to take on mythic proportions of his own. As the dividing lines between hero and anti-hero crumble, it is safe to say that Leopold Bloom now enjoys as great an epic stature among his modern admirers as his Greek counterpart ever did. ⟨. . .⟩

—Zack Bowen, "*Ulysses*" In *A Companion to Joyce Studies*, ed. Zack Bowen and James F. Carens (Westport, Connecticut: Greenwood Press, 1984): pp. 428–430.

JOSEPH C. HEININGER ON STEPHEN DEDALUS BETWEEN *PORTRAIT* AND *ULYSSES*

[In his essay from the Summer 1996 issue of the *James Joyce Quarterly* entitled "Stephen Dedalus in Paris: Tracing the

Fall of Icarus in *Ulysses*" Heininger looks closely at Stephen's remarks from conversations and silent monologue that reveal his state of mind in *Ulysses*.]

One of the major interpretive challenges confronting readers of the opening pages of *Ulysses* is to establish the relationship between the Stephen Dedalus of the close of *A Portrait of the Artist as a Young Man* and the Stephen of June 16, 1904. From the beginning, it is apparent that the weary Stephen we encounter on page three of *Ulysses* contrasts sharply with the hopeful and eager Stephen of the end of *A Portrait*. As *A Portrait* draws to a close, Stephen's diary entries record his preparations for leaving Ireland and his soaring, romantic declaration of Dedalian artistic purpose: "Welcome, O life! I go to encounter for the millionth time the reality of experience and to forge in the smithy of my soul the uncreated conscience of my race." As *Ulysses* opens, the "Telemachia" portrays a changed Stephen. By the morning of June 16, 1904, he seems to have become a frustrated, self-accusing and self-justifying young man, a would-be artist disillusioned by his recent encounters with the "reality of experience."

What has happened to Stephen in the thirteen-month interval between April 27, 1903 and June 16, 1904? We learn from reading the "Telemachia" that two significant experiences have affected Stephen's personality and plans: his mother's death and his two brief stays in Paris. ⟨. . .⟩

Joyce's handling of Stephen's memories of Paris in *Ulysses* allows us to see clearly that the young artist who went to Paris to encounter "the reality of experience" has instead learned there to distrust himself and to question his gifts. In "Scylla and Charybdis," Stephen reviews his experience of flight and return and calls himself a "lapwing" and "Icarus": "Fabulous artificer, the hawklike man. You flew. Whereto? Newhaven-Dieppe, steerage passenger. Paris and back. Lapwing. Icarus. *Pater, ait.* Seabedabbled, fallen, weltering. Lapwing you are. Lapwing he." As this self-assessment indicates, Stephen has not found in Paris any of the success he had hoped for but rather a series of political, artistic, religious, and sexual disillusionments. The "nets" he had tried to escape by leaving Ireland have demonstrated their universal reach and unexpected strength. The Paris of Stephen Dedalus, rather than the exciting center of intellectual and artistic life he had imagined, or the "gay Paree" of popular imagination, has been a hard check on his great expectations. A confident and as yet untested Dedalus had prepared to soar out of Ireland on the last page of *A Portrait,* but in *Ulysses* his flight to Paris has succeeded, however unintentionally and paradoxically, in entangling him in the "nets" of real experience.

The composite portrait of Stephen that emerges from *Ulysses* can be interpreted as that of a self-loathing artistic failure, as that of a sadder but wiser young man possessing still unrealized artistic gifts, or as indicating still other possibilities. Any careful, balanced view of Stephen Dedalus in *Ulysses* must depend on how one construes the meaning(s) of the evidence Joyce presents in the rest of the book, especially Stephen's "Parable of the Plums" and his eventual meeting with Leopold Bloom. Whatever nuances in Stephen's character may be suggested by the larger contexts of his story in *Ulysses,* Joyce has provided sufficient evidence within the narrative itself to demonstrate that Stephen's experiences in Paris have formed a pattern of frustrations to his hopes of personal distinction and artistic success.

—Joseph C. Heininger, "Stephen Dedalus in Paris: Tracing the Fall of Icarus in *Ulysses,*" *James Joyce Quarterly* 23, no. 4 (Summer 1986): pp. 435, 443–444.

Jasna Peručić-Nadarević on *Ulysses* as Comedy

[International attention to Joyce has become possible in recent years through the publication of several new translations. Jasna Peručić-Nadarević is a reader and critic of Joyce from Yugoslavia. These comments are from his chapter "*Ulysses* as Human Comedy" in *International Perspectives on James Joyce* (1986).]

In *Ulysses* Joyce himself became silent to allow the epic comedy of humanity to be heard. This withdrawal behind his handiwork makes the book less *personal* only that it may thus become all the more epically *human.* Joyce's work is clearly an example of imposed rather than organic form, for Joyce like Shakespeare, believes in *art* as specifically human and natural to human beings ("the art itself is nature.") The imposed form is in fact the aesthetic representative of the mode of *Ulysses*, comedy—which needs a degree of detachment—and indeed of a particular kind of comedy: in the last analysis, celebratory. The celebratory quality is embodied not only in the vitalist theme that leads to the final "yes." This theme is seen in the constant opposition of forces of life to those of death. The "life-force" theme can be found in the vitality expressed through the variety of styles, as well as in the vitality shown in each; formally in the many protean word-games; in Bloom's resilience and Molly's earth-mother characteristics, and even in Stephen's self-critical wit and ultimate injunction to hold on to "the now, the here"; and finally in the suggestion of the mythical systems running parallel with modern Dublin: thus continuity *and* change are shown to be fundamental to life. The essential human resilience that enables man to dodge or fight back is the condition for continual resurrections after the apparent triumph of death-forces. In other words, this vitality is found in structure, texture and character—indeed in the whole of that aspect of art which works in the service of life and is itself an expression of its creative energies.

Ulysses is "human" in three separate, though interrelated senses: as opposed to *divine,* to *inhuman,* and to *guiltless.* Thus, its comedy is universal, celebratory, and tolerant. *Ulysses* is firmly rooted in the secular world. There is a "coming down to earth," a bringing down of all that is highfalutin over-spiritual, ideal, abstract. For Joyce, the human spirit is always embodied in the particular, "the now, the here." However confused and imperfect the ordinary world may be, it is the world in which our values exist. Its confusions and imperfections, indeed, are the soil in which grow those humane values that *Ulysses* both portrays and embodies. Ulysses confirms that *Errare humanum est,* in other words, that nothing human should be alien to man. However ludicrous, the characters are seen as human, not monstrous in their faults, sufferings, and hopes.

—Jasna Peručić-Nadarević, "*Ulysses* as Human Comedy." In *International Perspectives on James Joyce,* Gaiser Gottlieb ed., (Troy, New York: Whitston Publishing Company, 1986): pp. 133–134.

[Brook Thomas is author of *James Joyce's* Ulysses: *A Book of
Many Happy Returns* (1982). He is in the department of
English at the University of California at Irvine and is interested in the relation of literary works to contemporary
political and social issues facing American culture. This
extract is from *The James Joyce Quarterly* (Spring 1986).]

⟨H⟩istory inhabits the *discours* of *Ulysses* in ways we do not always
notice—in its margins and gaps. We can see this at work by looking
at a passage in "Wandering Rocks."

Entering D.B.C., Mulligan and Haines first see John Howard Parnell, the brother of the famous Irish politician. Each orders a
melange, and Mulligan says, laughing:

> —We call it D.B.C. because they have damn bad cakes.
> O, but you missed Dedalus on *Hamlet.*
> Haines opened his newbought book.
> —I'm sorry, he said. Shakespeare is the happy hunting-
> ground of all minds that have lost their balance.
> The onelegged sailor growled at the area of 14 Nelson
> street:
> —*England expects . . .*
> Buck Mulligan's primrose waistcoat shook gaily to his
> laughter.

The brief flash to the onelegged sailor disrupts the flow of the narrative as it both defers Mulligan's response and creates a gap in the
text. We can try to fill that gap by remaining in the text and remembering that the sailor has appeared before. But to complete the
sailor's line we ultimately have to go to a world outside of the text.
Through a reference book we can find out that the song on the
sailor's mind is "The Death of Nelson," in which "England expects
that ev'ry man/This day will do his duty." That duty is, as we can
glean from the sailor's earlier appearance, to serve "England, home,
and beauty."

The irony of having a onelegged sailor think of such a patriotic
song is obvious, especially to an audience, like Joyce's original one,
that had a fresh memory of the human destruction brought about

by so many soldiers and sailors doing their duty in World War I. Less obvious is the ironic disruption that the sailor has on the exchange between Haines and Mulligan. The sailor's physical loss of balance from doing his duty for England complements the mental loss of balance of critics in service to England's master playwright. "Shakespeare is the happy huntingground of all minds that have lost their balance." Indeed, the Shakespeare theory that Haines missed is truly a theory about "England, home, and beauty," since Stephen interprets Shakespeare by linking the domestic life of England's most famous literary figure to his art. But if an Englishman's duty is to weave a harmonious unity between "England, home, and beauty," Irishman Stephen expounds a theory of art in which works are produced in the context of domestic strife. The duty of an Irish poet may well be to disrupt pious theories of English art.

⟨. . .⟩ We can sense how disruptive that turn in the narrative is if we imagine an Irish reader, one who would not have to go to a reference book to complete the sailor's line because his consciousness is full of English songs calling for him—an Irishman—to fulfill his duty to England. For such a reader the sailor's appearance opens the text to a historical world in which Dubliners' consciousnesses were shaped by British rule. In turn, through the reader's consciousness—one that we can reconstruct only by referring to other texts—the historical world of Dublin enters the text of *Ulysses* to interweave with its seemingly seamless narrative surface. Thus, at the very moment that the Irish reader fills in the line calling for every man to do his duty, the narrative moves forward to present Mulligan laughing at an Englishman's joke. Often considered unbalancing, Mulligan's laughter is here unbalanced, as it is shown to what extent it is in complicity with the conquering race. ⟨. . .⟩

—Brook Thomas, "History in the Margins of *Ulysses*," *The James Joyce Quarterly* 23, no. 3 (Spring 1986): pp. 360–361.

[Umberto Eco lectures on literature and semiotics at the University of Bologna in Italy. Eco sees Joyce as being at the node where the Middle Ages and the avant-garde meet and *Ulysses* as the place in history and consciousness where the world as a rational place gives way to chaos. This extract is taken from *The Aesthetics of Chaosmos: The Middle Ages of James Joyce* (1989).]

The traditional novel must disregard, for example, the fact that the protagonist blew his nose, unless the act means something from the point of view of the necessity of the plot. The act which does not "mean" is an insignificant and therefore a "stupid" one. With Joyce, we have the full acceptance of all the stupid acts of daily life as narrative material. The Aristotelian perspective is radically overturned. What was first inessential becomes the center of the action. Important things no longer happen in the novel, but an assortment of little things, without order, in an incoherent flow—thoughts and gestures, psychic associations as well as behavior automatisms.

This renouncement of the hierarchical organization of facts means eliminating the traditional conditions for judgment. In the "well made" novel the judgment exists by virtue of the plot. A plot proposes causal connections and thus explanations; it states that fact B happens because of fact A. When one tells a story using this narrative convention, one pretends *to tame history*. According to Aristotle, it is a question of eliminating the fortuitousness of "history" (the mere presence of *res gestae*) and joining it to the perspective of "poetry" (the organization of a *historia rerum gestarum*). On the contrary, *Ulysses* offers the choice of the *res gestae* against the *historia rerum gestarum*, of life against poetry, the indiscriminate use of all the events, renouncing of choice, the leveling of the insignificant fact next to the fact that counts. No fact is more or less significant than another fact; they all become weightless for they all have the same importance. ⟨. . .⟩

⟨. . .⟩ This situation brings to mind many discussions in contemporary psychology and epistemology. The problems that the novelist confronts in using such techniques are analogous to those that the philosopher encounters in redefining the concept of "personality," "individual consciousness," "perceptual field," etc. By decomposing thought and thus the traditional entity "mind" into the sum of individual "thoughts," the author faces both a crisis in narrative time and a crisis of the personage.

This problem emerges, however, only if we take the author's point of view in the construction of his sequences. From the reader's point of view the problem is easier. From the very moment that we are familiar with the narrative technique of *Ulysses*, we are able to isolate the various personages in the magma of voices, figures, ideas, and odors that constitute the general field of events. Not only do we individuate Bloom, Molly and Stephen, but we also manage to characterize and judge them. The reason is quite simple. Each personage is constituted by the same undifferentiated field of physical and mental events, yet each is united by a personal style of discourse. Bloom's stream assumes characteristics diverse from Stephen's and Stephen's stream differs from that of Molly. As the result of these stylistic solutions, the personages of *Ulysses* appear more alive, more complex and more individualized than those of any good traditional novel in which an omniscient author pauses to describe and explain every internal event of his hero.

—Umberto Eco, *The Aesthetics of Chaosmos: The Middle Ages of James Joyce* (Cambridge: Harvard University Press, 1989): pp. 39–40, 43.

CHRISTOPHER BUTLER ON JOYCE IN THE MODERNIST PERSPECTIVE

[Christopher Butler is Tutor in English Literature at Oxford. In 1984 he published *Interpretation, Deconstruction, and Ideology: An Introduction to Some Current Issues in Literary Theory*. In this extract from his essay in *The Cambridge Companion to James Joyce* (1990) Butler discusses the terms "modernism" and "postmodernism" and the way Joyce belongs—and does not belong—in the modernist perspective.]

⟨. . .⟩ First of all I look at his becoming 'modernist' in the most obvious sense—that is, by moving beyond his nineteenth-century predecessors. ⟨. . .⟩

Modernist artists at the beginning of the century were to a large degree moved to this unprecedented freedom and confidence in stylistic experiment by what they saw as radically new ideas, current in that period, concerning consciousness, time, and the nature of knowledge, which were to be found in the work of Nietzsche, Bergson, Freud, Einstein, Croce, Weber, and others. And these ideas contested in a dramatic manner the beliefs of the older generation. ⟨. . .⟩

Joyce's attitude to the modernist climate of ideas thus has largely to be inferred from his essentially solitary (and egotistical) experimentalism, and from our sense of the ideological risks it ran. For by the time he is writing *Ulysses* he has set himself the 'task' 'of writing a book from eighteen different points of view and in as many styles, all apparently unknown or undiscovered by my fellow tradesmen', and this stylistic diversity enshrines an essentially relativist attitude towards the 'truthful' depiction of reality. It makes an implicit stand against the ideological authority of the nineteenth-century novel, and of those other incorporative ideas which threatened him (as for example in the sermon of the *Portrait*). ⟨. . .⟩

Nevertheless Joyce's *resistance* to certain contemporary ideas is of equal importance. His philosophical allegiances are to the pre-moderns, for example to Aquinas, for even when he is subverting Catholic dogma, one can feel that so far as Stephen's aesthetic theories go, he believes that the Scholastics have at least correctly formulated the categories with which we have to think. ⟨. . .⟩

Joyce's extraordinary fidelity to past time thus means that the *ideas* he presents in his books are not those of the modernist avant-garde. It is through his style that modernism is implied. And so it is the stylistic innovations of the opening and closing pages of *A Portrait* which launch Joyce into an original modernist experimentalism which is almost wholly unpredictable in terms of these earlier influences. ⟨. . .⟩

It is the *ideology* of avant-garde movements which Joyce finds irrelevant to his purposes; and my judgement is that he quickly appropriated all available modernist techniques, while keeping himself well clear of the often inflated claims for 'simultaneity', the 'destruction of the past', and so on, of the manifestos.

> —Christopher Butler, "Joyce, Modernism, and Postmodernism." In *The Cambridge Companion to James Joyce,* Derek Attridge ed. (Cambridge: Cambridge University Press, 1990) pp. 259, 261, 265, 269.

ROBERT SPOO ON THE CACOPHONY OF WRITING STYLES IN "AEOLUS"

> [Robert Spoo is the editor of *The James Joyce Quarterly.* He is currently working on an edition of the letters of Ezra and Dorothy Pound. His book on Joyce, *James Joyce and the Language of History* was published in 1994. Spoo looks at the noisy competing voices in "Aeolus" and suggests one way to understand the apparent chaos.]

There are four major rhetorical pieces in "Aeolus"—Dan Dawson's effusion on Ireland, Seymour Bushe's address at the Childs murder trial, John F. Taylor's defense of Gaelic, and Stephen's Parable—each of which embodies specific assumptions about history and the relation of the past to the present. If we add Professor MacHugh's attack on the Roman (British) Empire, and Ignatius Gallaher's journalistic coup, we have two more rhetorical or para-rhetorical efforts, and there are others, including Bloom's Keyes ad and the newspaper captions Joyce added to the final version of the episode. But the first four are the most conspicuous and self-conscious, and they trace an ascending line of dignity and intensity which reaches its zenith in Taylor's piece and then seems to plunge bathetically with Stephen's Parable. ⟨...⟩

Critics have noted that as "Aeolus" progresses, the newspaper captions or headlines interspersed throughout the narrative seem to increase in frequency and fatuity. Beginning in Victorian propriety ("GENTLEMEN OF THE PRESS") and ending in a frightful jumble of tabloid high jinks ("SOME COLUMN!—THAT'S WHAT WADDLER ONE SAID"), the captions seem to sketch a history of journalistic styles ending in an explosive release of chaotic energies, not unlike the progress of literary styles in "Oxen of the Sun." Surely one reason for the aggressiveness of the captions at the end of "Aeolus" is that Stephen's Parable is as much a threat to journalism as journalism is to serious writing of the type to which he aspires. Stephen's counter-rhetoric, although it follows journalism in taking the city for its subject, is antithetical to the obliging windiness and winking familiarity of tabloid hype. As if recognizing this, the captions become more frenzied and turbulent as Stephen speaks, pursuing the Parable as if it were a foreign presence, clutching, as it were, at the escaping anti-Aeolian. We might compare Bloom's response when Stephen recites the Parable to him in "Ithaca." Ever the practical-minded entrepreneur, Bloom suggests that the piece might be collected with other essays in a volume of "model pedagogic themes" or "contributed in printed form, following the precedent of Philip Beaufoy or Doctor Dick or Heblon's *Studies in Blue.*" With the best intentions at heart, Bloom too would contain and neutralize the troubling counterdiscourse of Stephen's tale. Less well meaning, the "Aeolus" captions chase Stephen like the newsboys who heckle Bloom, "the last zig-zagging white on the breeze a mocking kite, a tail of white bowknots."

Despite this minor mutiny of the captions, the text of *Ulysses* eagerly takes up the contestatory project begun in Stephen's Parable. In "Ithaca" Bloom recalls the newspaper he was about to "throw away" that morning and how by means of it he unwittingly gave Bantam Lyons a tip on the horse Throwaway. Catechized about this coincidence, the text proudly affirms that Bloom "proceeded . . . with the light of inspiration shining in his countenance and bearing in his arms the secret of the race, graven in the language of prediction." This heavy-handed parody of John F. Taylor's speech accomplishes a demystification similar to the one Stephen's Parable seeks more indirectly. The phrase "secret of the race" challenges the whole ideology of the chosen Race that lies behind much of the rhetoric in the newspaper offices, particularly MacHugh's claims about the "spiritual" nature of the Irish. Joyce detested the nationalist doctrines of racial purity and cultural exclusiveness prevalent in Ireland at the turn of the century. This is why *Ulysses* keeps returning to the unexpected victory of the horse Throwaway, for it is an example of a "rank outsider," like Bloom, upsetting the "race." As Mr. Deasy's parting jest in "Nestor" implies, Bloom disturbs the "purity" of the race, and his reward is expulsion from Barney Kiernan's pub at the end of "Cyclops." While patriots were emphasizing the racial homogeneity of Ireland, Joyce remained faithful to a personal ideal of heterogeneity, which he expressed in the dense wovenness of his language and in the ironic ideological transactions of his historiographic art. "Aeolus" itself is a variegated tapestry of cultures—Irish, English, Jewish, Greek, Roman—and the rhetoric in the episode succeeds only in spreading heterogeneity and "impurity."

—Robert Spoo, *James Joyce and the Language of History* (New York: Oxford University Press, 1994): pp. 120–121, 130–131.

Zhao Mei on Joyce as Inspiration for Contemporary Chinese Readers

[Zhao Mei is a contemporary Chinese writer and literary critic. She has been writing since 1986 and her novels are noted for their realism and depth of feeling. They include *Lovers at the End of the Century* and *Lang Garden.* In this extract from an essay appearing in the Winter 1999 issue of *The James Joyce Quarterly,* Zhao Mei acknowledges the power of Joyce's writing for Chinese readers who have recently gained access to *Ulysses* through a 1986 translation by Jin Di.]

"Wandering Rocks" ⟨. . .⟩ is a courageous experiment in explicating the relationship between space and time. These nineteen sections constitute a cross-section of one single hour. Without a change in time, space is expanded; the extension of the scenes brings time to a stop. This is, in fact, not only confined to "Wandering Rocks" but applies to the whole work, since Joyce is really describing just a single day in Bloom's life. The reader sees the actions and events taking place in various corners of Dublin in words far more voluminous than those usually employed to describe a single day and reads the extremely rich and sensitive inner worlds of the characters. As a result, the novel transcends its words (which are, as a rule, linear) and assumes the qualities of a painting—but with a view more profound and stereoscopic. In short, it gives us an entirely new perspective.

What especially attracts my attention is also Joyce's avoidance of quotation marks for the conversations. Instead, he uses the dash to introduce a character's speech and places the narrative about the speaker in the context. It is a practice Joyce started in his earlier fiction. The following is an example:

> —What are you doing here, Stephen?
>> Dilly's high shoulders and shabby dress.
>> Shut the book quick. Don't let see.
>
> —What are you doing? Stephen said.

In these few short lines, we have not only the characters' words but also a description of their appearances, plus a depiction of the thoughts passing through their minds. In this way, free of the limitations of quotation marks, the author's pen constantly shifts freely between question, description, internal psychological activities, and reply. This allows the author's work to enter a realm of total freedom. The dialogue without quotation marks has greatly influenced Chinese writers, many of whom have adopted it. As for myself, ever since I began to engage in fiction-writing in 1986, I have not once used quotation marks for the dialogues in my books. It was Joyce who gave me the understanding that quotation marks are a kind of limitation. They destroy the true state of reality. Particularly when dialogue, action, and mental activity are simultaneous, you cannot use quotation marks to show the true condition of real life. We must, therefore, discard them; we must break through the limitations that they impose on a dynamic status.

We have also begun to consider whether the usual episodes, sections, paragraphs, and punctuation marks stand in the way of our description. I personally have been experimenting in those respects. For example, when I need to show a very strong emotion, I resort to a long sentence without any punctuation. Sometimes I write a number of broken sentences in a row or a succession of very short sentences with only a few words each. I employ repeated use of the full stop or just one or two words to indicate an action or idea. Sometimes I deliberately lump a character's words, actions, and inner thoughts into one sentence. The subject of the sentence changes continuously in its depths in order to conduct the multiple levels of the person's activity within the twinkling of an eye. All these experimental techniques have been inspired by Joyce. ⟨. . .⟩

This stream-of-consciousness technique of Joyce's has recently been widely adopted in Chinese literature, especially among avant-garde writers. They even go beyond Joyce in that their stream-of-consciousness becomes even more abrupt and irregular. Some resemble the delirium of a psychotic.

What we, as Chinese writers, get from reading Joyce's *Ulysses*, I believe, is a realization that there are limitless possibilities for creative methods. ⟨. . .⟩

—Zhao Mei, "Joyce's Influence on Contemporary Chinese Writers," *The James Joyce Quarterly* 36, no. 2 (Winter 1999): pp. 282–283, 284–285.

Works by
James Joyce

Chamber Music. 1907.

Dubliners. 1914.

A Portrait of the Artist as a Young Man. 1916.

Exiles: A Play in Three Acts. 1918.

Ulysses. 1922.

Pomes Penyeach. 1927.

James Clarence Mangan. 1930.

Ibsen's New Play. 1930.

Collected Poems. 1936.

Finnegans Wake. 1939.

Pastimes. 1941.

Introducing James Joyce: A Selection from Joyce's Prose. Ed. T. S. Eliot. 1942.

Stephen Hero: Part of the First Draft of A Portrait of the Artist as a Young Man. Ed. Theodore Spencer. 1944.

The Portable James Joyce. Ed. Harry Levin. 1947.

The Early Joyce: The Book Reviews 1902–03. Ed. Stanislaus Joyce and Ellsworth Mason. 1955.

Epiphanies. Ed. O. A. Silverman. 1956.

Letters. Ed. Stuart Gilbert and Richard Ellmann. 1957–66.

Critical Writings. Ed. Ellsworth Mason and Richard Ellmann. 1959.

Scribbledehobble: The Ur-Workbook for Finnegans Wake. Ed. Thomas Connolly. 1961.

The Cat and the Devil. 1964

Works About James Joyce

Adams, Robert Martin. *After Joyce: Studies in Fiction After* Ulysses. New York: Oxford University Press, 1977.

Almeida, Hermione ed. *Byron and Joyce Through Homer:* Don Juan *and* Ulysses. New York: Columbia University Press, 1981.

————. *James Joyce and His World.* London: Thames & Hudson, 1967.

Arnold, Armin, and Judy Young. *James Joyce.* New York: Ungar, 1969.

Arnold, Bruce. *The Scandal of* Ulysses. New York: St. Martin's Press, 1991.

Attridge, Derek. *Peculiar Language: Literature as Difference from the Renaissance to James Joyce.* Ithaca: Cornell University Press, 1988.

————. *The Cambridge Companion to James Joyce.* Cambridge: Cambridge University Press, 1990.

Attridge, Derek, and Daniel Ferrer. *Post-Structuralist Joyce: Essays from the French.* Cambridge: Cambridge University Press, 1984.

Bauerle, Ruth. *Picking Up Airs: Hearing the Music in Joyce's Text.* Urbana: University of Illinois Press, 1993.

Beckett, Samuel, et al. *Our Exagmination Round His Factification for Incamination of Work in Progress.* 1929. New York: New Directions, 1972.

Begnal, Michael, and Fritz Senn. *A Conceptual Guide to Finnegans Wake.* University Park, Pennsylvania: Pennsylvania State University Press, 1974.

Beja, Morris. *James Joyce,* Dubliners *and* A Portrait of the Artist as a Young Man: *A Selection of Critical Essays.* London: Macmillan, 1973.

————. *James Joyce: A Literary Life.* Columbus: Ohio State University Press, 1992.

Bell, Robert H. *Jocoserious Joyce: The Fate of Folly in* Ulysses. Ithaca: Cornell University Press, 1991.

Ben Merre, Diana A., and Maureen Murphy. *James Joyce and His Contemporaries.* Westport, Connecticut: Greenwood, 1989.

Benstock, Bernard. *Joyce-Again's Wake: An Analysis of* Finnegans Wake. Seattle: University of Washington Press, 1966.

———. *The Seventh of Joyce.* Bloomington; Brighton: Indiana University Press; Harvester, 1982.

———. *James Joyce.* New York: Ungar, 1985.

———. *Critical Essays on James Joyce's* Ulysses. Boston: G. K. Hall, 1989.

———. *Narrative Con/Texts in* Ulysses. Urbana: University of Illinois Press, 1991.

Benstock, Bernard, and Thomas F. Staley (ed.). *Approaches to Joyce's Portrait: Ten Essays.* Pittsburgh: University Pittsburgh Press, 1976.

Benstock, Shari, and Bernard Benstock. *Who's He When He's at Home: A James Joyce Directory.* Chicago: University of Illinois Press, 1980.

Blamires, Harry. *The Bloomsday Book: A Guide through Joyce's* Ulysses. London: Methuen, 1966.

Bloom, Harold. *James Joyce.* New York: Chelsea, 1986.

———. *James Joyce's "Ulysses".* New York: Chelsea, 1987.

———. *James Joyce's "Dubliners".* New York: Chelsea, 1988.

———. *James Joyce's "A Portrait of the Artist as a Young Man".* New York: Chelsea, 1988.

Bonheim, Helmut. *Joyce's Benefictions.* Berkeley: University of California Press, 1964.

Bowen, Zack. *Musical Allusions in the Works of James Joyce: Early Poetry Through* Ulysses. Albany, New York: S.U.N.Y. Press, 1974.

———. *Bloom's Old Sweet Song: Essays on Joyce and Music.* Gainesville: University Press of Florida, 1995.

Bowen, Zack, and James F. Carens. *A Companion to Joyce Studies.* Westport, Connecticut: Greenwood, 1984.

Bradley, Bruce S. J., and Richard Ellmann. *James Joyce's Schooldays.* New York: St. Martin's, 1982.

Brandabur, Edward. *A Scrupulous Meanness: A Study of Joyce's Early Work.* Urbana: University of Illinois Press, 1971.

Brivic, Sheldon. *Joyce Between Freud and Jung.* Port Washington: Kennikat, 1980.

———. *Joyce the Creator.* Madison: University of Wisconsin Press, 1985.

———. *The Veil of Signs: Joyce, Lacan, and Perception.* Urbana: University of Illinois Press, 1991.

Budgen, Frank. *James Joyce and the Making of* Ulysses, *and Other Writings.* 1934. London: Oxford University Press, 1972.

Burgess, Anthony. *Joysprick: An Introduction to the Language of James Joyce.* London: Deutsch.

———. *Here Comes Everybody: An Introduction to James Joyce for the Ordinary Reader.* London: Faber, 1965.

Cato, Bob, and Greg Vitiello. *Joyce Images.* With an Introduction by Anthony Burgess. New York: Norton, 1994.

Cheng, Vincent J. *Joyce, Race, and Empire.* Cambridge: Cambridge University Press, 1995.

Cheng, Vincent J., and Timothy Martin. *Joyce in Context.* Cambridge, England: Cambridge University Press, 1992.

Costello, Peter. *James Joyce: The Years of Growth (1882–1915).* New York: Pantheon, 1992.

Culleton, Claire A. *Names and Naming in Joyce.* Madison: University of Wisconsin Press, 1994.

Curran, Constantine. *James Joyce Remembered.* New York: Oxford University Press, 1968.

Dent, R. W. *Colloquial Language in* Ulysses: *A Reference Tool.* Newark; London: University of Delaware Press; Associated University Press, 1994.

Driver, Clive, and Harry Levin. *James Joyce's* Ulysses: *A Facsimile of the Manuscript; 2 Vols.* New York: Octagon, 1976.

Duffy, Enda. *The Subaltern Ulysses.* Minneapolis: University of Minneapolis, 1994.

Dunleavy, Janet, ed. *Re-viewing Classics of Joyce Criticism.* Urbana: University of Illinois Press, 1991.

Eco, Umberto. *The Aesthetics of Chaosmos: The Middle Ages of James Joyce.* Trans. Ellen Esrock and David Robey. Cambridge: Harvard University Press, 1989.

Ehrlich, Heyward. *Light Rays: James Joyce and Modernism.* New York: New Horizon, 1984.

Ellmann, Richard. *Yeats and Joyce*. Dublin: Dolmen Press, 1967.

———. *Eminent Domain: Yeats Among Wilde, Joyce, Pound, Eliot and Auden*. London and New York: Oxford University Press, 1970.

———. *Selected Letters of James Joyce*. New York: Viking, 1975.

———. *The Consciousness of Joyce*. Toronto: Oxford University Press, 1977.

———. *James Joyce*. 2nd Ed. 1959. New York: Oxford University Press, 1982.

———. *Ulysses on the Liffey*. New York: Oxford University Press, 1979.

Epstein, Edmund L. *The Ordeal of Stephen Dedalus: The Conflict of the Generations in James Joyce's* A Portrait of the Artist as a Young Man. Carbondale: Southern Illinois University Press, 1973.

Fairhall, James. *James Joyce and the Question of History*. Cambridge: Cambridge University Press, 1993.

Ferris, Kathleen. *James Joyce and the Burden of Disease*. Lexington: University Kentucky Press, 1995.

Fogel, Daniel Mark. *Covert Relations: James Joyce, Virginia Woolf, and Henry James*. Charlottesville: University Press of Virginia, 1990.

French, Marilyn. *The Book as World: James Joyce's* Ulysses. Cambridge: Harvard University Press, 1976.

Freund, Gisele, V. B. Carleton, and Simone de Beauvoir. *James Joyce in Paris: His Final Years*. London: Cassell, 1966.

Friedman, Susan Stanford. Joyce: *The Return of the Repressed*. Ithaca: Cornell University Press, 1993.

Froula, Christine. *Modernism's Body: Sex, Culture and Joyce*. New York: Columbia University Press, 1996.

Gabler, Hans Walter, et al. Ulysses: *The Corrected Text*. New York: Random House, 1986.

Gaiser, Gottlieb. *International Perspectives on James Joyce*. Troy, New York: Whitston, 1986.

Garrett, Peter K. *Scene and Symbol from George Eliot to James Joyce: Studies in Changing Fictional Mode*. New Haven: Yale University Press, 1969.

Gaskill, Philip, et al. Ulysses: *A Review of Three Texts: Proposals for Alterations to the Texts of 1922, 1961, and 1984*. Gerards Cross: Colin Smythe, 1989.

Gifford, Don, and Robert J. Seidman. Ulysses *Annotated: Notes for James Joyce's* Ulysses. Rev. Ed. Berkeley: University of California Press, 1988.

Gifford, Don C. *Notes for Joyce: An Annotation of James Joyce's Ulysses.* New York: Dutton, 1974.

Gilbert, Stuart. *James Joyce's* Ulysses. 1930. New York: Knopf, 1952.

Gilbert, Stuart, and Richard Ellmann. *Letters; Vols. I, II, III.* New York: Viking, 1966.

Gillespie, Michael Patrick. *Inverted Volumes Improperly Arranged: James Joyce and His Trieste Library.* Ann Arbor: UMI Research Press, 1983.

———. *Reading the Book of Himself: Narrative Strategies in the Works of James Joyce.* Columbus: Ohio State University Press, 1989.

——— and A. Nicholas Fargnoli. *James Joyce A to Z.* New York: Facts on File, 1995 (hardback). New York: Oxford University Press, 1996 (paper).

Givens, Seon. *James Joyce: Two Decades of Criticism; With a New Introduction.* New York: Vanguard, 1963.

Gluck, Barbara Reich. *Beckett and Joyce: Friendship and Fiction.* Lewisburg: Bucknell University Press, London:Associated University Press.

Goldberg, S. L. *James Joyce.* Edinburgh; New York: Oliver & Boyd, 1963.

Goldman, Arnold. *James Joyce.* London; New York: Routledge, 1968.

Gorman, Herbert. *James Joyce: A Definitive Biography.* New York: Farrar & Rinehart, 1939.

Gose, Elliott B., Jr. *The Transformation Process in Joyce's* Ulysses. Toronto: University of Toronto Press, 1980.

Gottfried, Roy. *Joyce's Iritis and the Irritated Text: The Dis-Lexic Ulysses.* Gainesville: University Press of Florida,1995.

———. *The Art of Joyce's Syntax in* Ulysses. Athens: University of Georgia Press, 1980.

Groden, Michael. *Ulysses in Progress.* Princeton: Princeton University Press, 1977.

Grose, Kenneth. *James Joyce.* London: Evans, 1975.

Gross, John. *James Joyce.* New York: Viking, 1970.

Gunn, Ian, Alistair McCleery, and A. Walton Litz. *The* Ulysses *Pagefinder.* Edinburgh: Split Pea, 1988.

Halper, Nathan. *The Early James Joyce*. New York and London: Columbia University Press, 1973.

Hancock, Leslie. *Word Index to James Joyce's* Portrait of the Artist. Carbondale; London: Southern Illinois University Press, 1967.

Hanley, Miles L., et al. *Word Index to James Joyce's* Ulysses. Madison: University Wisconsin Press, 1937. Note: Reprinted 1965. Concordance to the Random House edition.

Harper, Margaret Mills. *The Aristocracy of Art in Joyce and Wolfe*. Baton Rouge: Louisiana State University Press, 1990.

Hart, Clive. *Structure and Motif in Finnegans Wake*. Evanston: Northwest University Press, 1962.

———. *James Joyce's* Ulysses. University Park; Sydney; London: Pennsylvania State University Press, 1968.

———. *James Joyce's* Dubliners: *Critical Essays*. New York: Viking, 1969.

———. *A Concordance to* Finnegans Wake. Mamaroneck, New York: Appel, 1974.

———. *Conversations with James Joyce (by) Arthur Power*. London: Millington, 1974.

Hart, Clive, and Fritz Senn. *A Wake Digest*. Sydney: Sydney University Press, 1968.

Hart, Clive, and C. George Sandulescu. *Assessing the 1984 Ulysses*. Gerrards Cross: Barnes and Noble, 1986.

Harty, John. *James Joyce's* Finnegans Wake. New York: Garland, 1991.

Hayman, David. Ulysses: *The Mechanics of Meaning*. New Ed., Revised & Expanded. Madison: University of Wisconsin Press, 1982.

Heller, Vivian. *Joyce, Decadence, and Emancipation*. Urbana: University of Illinois Press, 1995.

Henke, Suzette A. *Joyce's Moraculous Sindbook: A Study of* Ulysses. Columbus: Ohio State University Press, 1978.

———. *James Joyce and the Politics of Desire*. New York: Routledge, 1990.

Henke, Suzette, Elaine Unkeless, and Carolyn G. Heilbrun. *Women in Joyce*. Urbana: University of Illinois Press,1982.

Herr, Cheryl. Joyce's *Anatomy of Culture*. Urbana: University of Illinois Press, 1986.

Herring, Phillip F. *Joyce's* Ulysses *Notesheets in the British Museum.* Charlottesville: University Press of Virginia for the Bibliog. Soc., 1972.

———. *Joyce's Notes and Early Drafts for* Ulysses: *Selections from the Buffalo Collection.* Charlottesville: University Press of Virginia, 1975.

———. *Joyce's Uncertainty Principle.* Princeton: Princeton University Press, 1987.

Hofheinz, Thomas C. *Joyce and the Invention of Irish History:* Finnegans Wake *in Context.* Cambridge: Cambridge University Press, 1995.

Hogan, Patrick Colm. *Joyce, Milton and the Theory of Influence.* Gainesville: University Press of Florida, 1995.

Houston, John Porter. *Joyce and Prose: An Exploration of the Language of* Ulysses. Lewisburg, Pennsylvania: Bucknell University Press, 1989.

Ingersoll, Earl G. *Engendered Trope in Joyce's* Dubliners. Carbondale: Southern Illinois University Press, 1996.

Jackson, Selwyn. *The Poems of James Joyce and the Use of Poems in His Novels.* Frankfort, Kentucky: Lang, 1978.

Jackson, Tony E. *The Subject of Modernism: Narrative Alterations in the Fiction of Eliot, Conrad, Woolf, and Joyce.* Ann Arbor: University of Michigan Press, 1994.

Jones, William Powell. *James Joyce and the Common Reader.* Norman: University Oklahoma Press, 1955.

Kelly, Dermot. *Narrative Strategies in Joyce's* Ulysses. Ann Arbor: University Microfilms International Research Press, 1988.

Kenner, Hugh. *Dublin's Joyce.* London: Chatto & Windus, 1955.

———. *Joyce's Voices.* London: Faber & Faber, 1978.

———. *Ulysses.* Rev. ed. Baltimore: Johns Hopkins University Press, 1987.

Kershner, R. B. *James Joyce:* A Portrait of the Artist as a Young Man: *Complete, Authoritative Text with Biographical and Historical Contexts, Critical History, and Essays from Five Contemporary Critical Perspectives.* Boston: Bedford; St. Martin's, 1993.

Kershner, R. B. (ed. & introd.). *Joyce and Popular Culture.* Gainesville: University Press of Florida, 1996.

Litz, A. Walton. *The Art of James Joyce: Method and Design in* Ulysses *and* Finnegans Wake. Rev. ed. London: Oxford University Press, 1964.

———. *James Joyce*. New York: Twayne, 1966.

MacCabe, Colin. *James Joyce and the Revolution of the Word*. New York: Barnes and Noble, 1979.

———. *James Joyce: New Perspectives*. Brighton, England; Bloomington: Harvester; Indiana University Press,1982.

Maddox, Brenda. *Nora: A Biography of Nora Joyce*. London: Hamilton, 1988. Note: US title: *Nora: The Real Life of Molly Bloom*. Boston: Houghton Mifflin, 1988.

Maddox, James H. *Joyce's Ulysses and the Assault upon Character*. New Brunswick: Rutgers University Press, 1978.

Magalaner, Marvin. *Critical Reviews of* A Portrait of the Artist as a Young Man. New York: PocketBooks, 1965.

Mahaffey, Vicki. *Reauthorizing Joyce*. Cambridge: Cambridge University Press, 1988.

Martin, Augustine. *James Joyce: The Artist and the Labyrinth*. London: Ryan, 1990.

Martin, Timothy. *Joyce and Wagner: A Study of Influence*. Cambridge, England: Cambridge University Press, 1991.

Mason, Michael. *James Joyce:* Ulysses. London: E. Arnold, 1972.

McCarthy, Patrick A. Ulysses: *Portals of Discovery*. Boston: Twayne, 1990.

———. *Critical Essays on James Joyce's* Finnegans Wake. New York: G. K. Hall, 1992.

McCormack, W. J., and Alistair Stead. *James Joyce and Modern Literature*. London: Routledge, 1982.

McCormick, Kathleen, and Erwin R. Steinberg. *Approaches to Teaching Joyce's* Ulysses. New York: Mod. Lang. Assn. of Amer., 1993.

McGrory, Kathleen, and John Unterecker. *Yeats, Joyce, and Beckett: New Light on Three Modern Irish Writers*. Lewisburg: Bucknell University Press, London: Associated University Press.

Mitchell, Breon. *James Joyce and the German Novel 1922–1933*. Athens: Ohio University Press, 1976.

Murillo, J. A. *The Cyclical Night: Irony in James Joyce and Jorge Luis Borges*. Cambridge: Harvard University Press, 1968.

Nadel, Ira B. *Joyce and the Jews: Culture and Texts.* Iowa City: University of Iowa Press, 1989.

Newman, Robert D., and Weldon Thornton. *Joyce's Ulysses: The Larger Perspective.* Newark: University of Delaware Press, 1987.

Nolan, Emer. *James Joyce and Nationalism.* London: Routledge, 1995.

Norris, David, and Carl Flint. *Introducing Joyce.* New York: Totem, 1994.

Norris, Margot. *Joyce's Web: The Social Unraveling of Modernism.* Austin: University of Texas Press, 1992.

O'Brien, Darcy. *The Conscience of James Joyce.* Princeton: Princeton University Press, 1968.

O'Connor, Ulick, et al. *The Joyce We Knew.* Cork: Mercier, 1967.

O'Shea, Michael J. *James Joyce and Heraldry.* Albany State University of New York Press, 1986.

Oates, Joyce Carol. *New Heaven, New Earth: The Visionary Experience in Literature.* New York: Vanguard, 1974.

Osteen, Mark. *The Economy of Ulysses: Making Both Ends Meet.* Syracuse, New York: Syracuse University Press, 1995.

Peake, C. H. *James Joyce: The Citizen and the Artist.* Stanford: Stanford University Press, 1977.

Pearl, Cyril. *Dublin in Bloomtime: The City James Joyce Knew.* New York; London: Viking, 1969.

Perelman, Bob. *The Trouble with Genius: Reading Pound, Joyce, Stein and Zukofsky.* Berkeley: University of California Press, 1994.

Potts, Willard, and Paul Ruggiero. *Portraits of the Artist in Exile: Recollections of James Joyce by Europeans.* Seattle: University of Washington Press, 1979.

Power, Arthur R. *Conversations with James Joyce.* New York: Barnes & Noble, 1974.

Read, Forrest. *Pound/Joyce: Letters & Essays; With Introduction & Commentary.* New York: New Directions,1967.

Restuccia, Frances L. *Joyce and the Law of the Father.* New Haven: Yale University Press, 1989.

Reynolds, Mary T. *Joyce and Dante: The Shaping Imagination.* Princeton: Princeton University Press, 1981.

———. *James Joyce: A Collection of Critical Essays.* Englewood Cliffs, New Jersey: Prentice Hall, 1993.

Riqueline, John Paul. *Teller and Tale in Joyce's Fiction: Oscillating Perspectives.* Baltimore: Johns Hopkins University Press, 1983.

Rose, Danis, John O'Hanlon, and Hans Walter Gabler. *The Lost Notebook: New Evidence on the Genesis of Ulysses.* Edinburgh: Split Pea, 1989.

Roughley, Alan. *James Joyce and Critical Theory: An Introduction.* Ann Arbor: University of Michigan Press, 1991.

Scholes, Robert, and Richard M. Kain. *The Workshop of Daedalus: James Joyce and the Raw Materials for* A Portrait of the Artist as a Young Man. Evanston: Northwestern University Press, 1965.

Scholes, Robert, and A. Walton Litz. Dubliners: *Text, Criticism, and Notes.* New York: Viking, 1969.

Schwarz, Daniel R. *Reading Joyce's* Ulysses. New York: St. Martin's, 1987.

———. *James Joyce:* The Dead. Boston: Bedford, 1994.

Scott, Bonnie Kime. *James Joyce.* Atlantic Highlands, New Jersey: Humanities Press, 1987.

———. *New Alliances in Joyce Studies: "When it's aped to foul a Delfian".* Newark: University of Delaware Press, 1988.

Seed, David. *James Joyce's* A Portrait of the Artist as a Young Man. New York: St. Martin's, 1992.

Segall, Jeffrey. *Joyce in America: Cultural Politics and the Trials of Ulysses.* Berkeley: University of California Press, 1993.

Seidel, Michael, and Thomas Crawford. *Epic Geography: James Joyce's* Ulysses: *Maps Drawn by Thomas Crawford.* Princeton: Princeton University Press, 1976.

Senn, Fritz. *New Light on Joyce from the Dublin Symposium.* Bloomington: Indiana University Press, 1972.

Senn, Fritz, and Christine O'Neill. *Inductive Scrutinies: Focus on Joyce.* Baltimore: Johns Hopkins University Press, 1995.

Senn, Fritz, and John Paul Riquelme. *Joyce's Dislocutions: Essays on Reading as Translation.* Baltimore: Johns Hopkins University Press, 1984.

Shechner, Mark. *Joyce in Nighttown: A Psychoanalytic Inquiry into* Ulysses. Berkeley: University of California Press, 1974.

Sherry, Vincent. *James Joyce/Ulysses.* Cambridge: Cambridge University Press, 1994.

Slocum, John, and Herbert Cahoon. *A Bibliography of James Joyce.* New Haven: Yale University Press, 1953.

Staley, Thomas F. *James Joyce Today: Essays on the Major Works.* Bloomington: Indiana University Press, 1966.

————. *An Annotated Critical Bibliography of James Joyce.* New York: St. Martin's, 1989.

Steinberg, Erwin R. *The Stream of Consciousness and Beyond in* Ulysses. Pittsburgh: University of Pittsburgh Press,1973.

Sultan, Stanley. *The Argument of Ulysses.* Columbus: Ohio State University Press, 1965.

————. *Ulysses, The Waste Land, and Modernism: A Jubilee Study.* Port Washington, New York: Kennikat, 1976.

Theall, Donald F. *Beyond the Word: Reconstructing Sense in the Joyce Era of Technology, Culture, and Communication.* Toronto: University of Toronto Press, 1995.

Theoharis, Theoharis Constantine. *Joyce's* Ulysses: *An Anatomy of the Soul.* Chapel Hill: University of North Carolina Press, 1988.

Thornton, Weldon. *Allusions in* Ulysses: *An Annotated List.* Chapel Hill: University of North Carolina Press, 1968.

————. *The Antimodernism of Joyce's* A Portrait of the Artist as a Young Man. Syracuse: Syracuse University Press, 1994.

Tindall, William York. *James Joyce: His Way of Interpreting the Modern World.* New York: Scribner, 1950.

————. *A Reader's Guide to James Joyce.* New York: Noonday Press, 1959.

————. *The Joyce Country.* New York: Schocken, 1972.

Tucker, Lindsey. *Stephen and Bloom at Life's Feast: Alimentary Symbolism and the Creative Process in James Joyce's* Ulysses. Columbus: Ohio State University Press, 1984.

Valente, Joseph. *James Joyce and the Problem of Justice: Negotiating Sexual and Colonial Difference.* Cambridge: Cambridge University Press, 1995.

Van Caspel, Paul. *Bloomers on the Liffey: Eisegetical Readings of Joyce's* Ulysses. Baltimore: Johns Hopkins University Press, 1986.

Warner, John M. *Joyce's Grandfathers: Myth and History in Defoe, Smollett, Sterne and Joyce.* Athens: University of Georgia Press, 1993.

Weir, Lorraine. *Writing Joyce: A Semiotics of the Joyce System.* Bloomington: Indiana University Press, 1989.

Weldon, Thorton. *Allusions in* Ulysses. Chapel Hill: University North Carolina Press, 1968.

Woronzoff, Alexander. *Andrej Belyj's Petersburg, James Joyce's Ulysses, and the Symbolist Movement.* Berne: Lang, 1982.

Index of
Themes and Ideas

CHAMBER MUSIC, 49, 50

DUBLINERS, THE, 14, 32, 34, 49, 50

FINNEGAN'S WAKE, 14, 52

JOYCE, JAMES: biography of, 12–15; framework for reading, 25–26

PORTRAIT OF THE ARTIST AS A YOUNG MAN, A, 14, 16–58; Father Arnall in, 24, 38, 40–41; John Casey in, 19; Catholic education in, 19, 20, 38; Catholicism in, 18, 19, 20, 21, 27, 28, 40–41, 54; characters in, 23–24; Uncle Charles in, 19, 23; Christmas dinner in, 19; claims on Stephen's soul in, 22, 32–33; Emma Cleary (E.C.) in, 24, 46; Father Conmee in, 19, 39; Cranley, Lynch, Heron, Davin in, 24, 27, 33; critical reception of, 16; critical views on, 9–10, 25–58; Simon Dedalus in, 17–18, 19, 20, 23, 31, 46–47, 53; Stephen Dedalus in, 9–10, 16–21, 23, 27–33, 35, 36–58, 91–93, *See also under* Stephen, *below;* Father Dolan in, 19, 20, 24, 38, 39; epiphany in, 21–22, 46, 49–51; "foetus" in, 16, 46–47; friendship in, 35; goats in, 37; green place in, 53; Irish history in, 30–32; Joyce's view of personality of writer in, 51–53; meaning of title of, 16; and Modernism, 44–45, 50, 99; moon in, 54; as objective autobiography, 26–28; oscillations in style and narrative in, 47–48; plot summary of, 16–22; politics in, 18, 81; Dante Riordan in, 18, 19, 23–24, 38; Nasty Roche in, 18; rose in, 52, 53; sacred and profane language in, 36–37; sea in, 36; sermon's impact on Stephen's mind in, 36, 40–41, 99; Stephen and time in, 18–19; Stephen as artist in, 28–30; Stephen as both god and devil in, 35; Stephen as outsider in, 18, 20, 21, 31; Stephen's artistic inclination in, 17–18, 52; Stephen's beating in, 19, 20, 38, 39; Stephen's effort to position himself in universe in, 16–17; Stephen's first words uttered in, 51–53; Stephen's impulse to escape in, 18, 27–28, 32–33, 43; Stephen's Irish background in, 30–32; Stephen's mother in, 18, 46–47; Stephen's mythic and heroic association in, 53–54; Stephen's name in, 28–29; Stephen's obstacles to becoming artist in, 43–45; Stephen's personality in, 41–43; Stephen's relation to women in Freudian context in, 38–39; Stephen's remembering thoughts in connection with places in, 55–56; Stephen's responsiveness to words and power of language in, 57–58; Stephen's sexuality in, 20–21, 27, 36–37, 46–47, 57–58, 79–80; Stephen's speculating about theology and metaphysics in, 17; Stephen's vision of heaven and hell in, 36–37; Stephen's vividness in, 9–10; women as enabler of male development in, 45–47